EARTH PONDS *Sourcebook*

EARTH PONDS *Sourcebook*

THE POND OWNER'S MANUAL AND RESOURCE GUIDE

TIM MATSON

THE COUNTRYMAN PRESS WOODSTOCK, VERMONT

First Edition 1997

Grateful acknowledgment is made to the following for permission to reprint previously published material: *The Journal of Light Construction;* The Minnesota Department of Natural Resources, for material from Carrol L. Henderson's *Woodworking for Wildlife;* Gene W. Wood, Department of Agriculture, Fisheries, and Wildlife, Clemson University; Elayne Sears, Frank Fretz and Vince Babek; Bow Bends; and Lilypons Water Gardens. Special thanks to the Kenyon Construction Company for permission to use images from their pond video.

Library of Congress Cataloging-in-Publication Data
Matson, Tim

Earth ponds sourcebook : the pond owner's manual and resource guide / Tim Matson.
p. cm.
Includes bibliographical references and index.
ISBN 0-88150-358-4 (alk. paper)
1. Water-supply, Rural—Amateurs' manuals. 2. Ponds—Design and construction—Amateurs' manuals. I. Title.
TD927.M436 1997
627'.14—dc21 97-10388
CIP

Published by The Countryman Press, PO Box 748, Woodstock, VT 05091
Distributed by W. W. Norton & Company, Inc., 500 Fifth Avenue, New York, NY 10110

Cover and text design by Ann Aspell
Cover and interior photographs by the author unless credited otherwise

Printed in the United States of America
10 9 8 7 6

ACKNOWLEDGMENTS

This book distills years of aquacultural experience and research, and countless conversations and visits with dozens of people. The following people deserve special credit for contributing to the project: Phyllis Bellmore, Jim Condict, Bob Drake, Noel Dydo, George Denagy, Ruth and John Dwyer, Dr. Jay Huner, Brian Kenyon, Ted Kenyon, Anna Kristensen, Bruce Keller, Stuart McComas, Flo and Joe Morse, Llama Lettow, Sean Mullen, Alan Moats, Helen Nash, John Rogers, Donny Prescott, Patrick Rusz, Sherm Stebbins, Gerard and Sandy Stevens, Blake and Aletta Traendly, Charles B. Thomas, Sardar Thanhauser, Louis Warlick, George Williams, Gene W. Wood, and Carrol L. Henderson.

I'd like to thank the editors of the following magazines, which originally published some of the material, in slightly different form: *Country Journal, Harrowsmith Country Life, Mother Earth News, The Journal of Light Construction, Tree Farmer,* and *Fine Homebuilding.* And, finally, special thanks to Ann Aspell, who designed the book; Gail Vernazza, whose good humor and word-processing skills made countless revisions an agreeable task; my brother Jonathan Matson, who represented the book with upbeat spirit and excellent counsel; and Helen Whybrow, my editor, unflappable and uncommonly patient, who brought it all together.

To my daughters,
Johanna Langtree Matson and Mayellen Elizabeth Matson,
with love.

CONTENTS

INTRODUCTION

What could be more primitive than digging a hole in the earth and filling it with water? That something so crude should yield so many rewards seems downright magical, and indeed pond building is a kind of alchemy, transforming the basic elements of earth and groundwater into liquid gold—that is, a reservoir of open water to treasure as drought and fire protection, wildlife habitat, recreation area, fishpond, skating rink, lily pond, and more.

The word *pond* derives from *impoundment,* "to hold," and I suspect that ponds satisfy a basic human urge to do just that, to possess water—to actually see it close by. After all, without it we die. On some primitive level a pond tells us to relax, that everything's okay, the essentials are here. Again, we have a primitive itch getting a very satisfying scratch.

On a more practical level, pond building works because it offers so much in so little space, for a price that's within reach. If you can't afford a $10,000 recreational fishpond, how about spending a couple of hundred dollars on a goldfish and lily pool? Both big ponds and small offer the aesthetic rewards of a liquid landscape, which can have a dramatic effect on the land (and land value) as well as the landowner. The tranquilizing effect of water may be in itself enough to justify a pond project. Add an after-work swim and a fishing lesson with your kids, and it's easy to fathom the lure of a homemade waterfront.

Consider yourself fortunate. You live in an age when for the first time it's relatively easy to add water to your yard and keep it there, whether by virtue of a favorable water table and the use of a hydraulic excavator, or by using the faucet and a plastic pool liner. Across the country, plant suppliers, wetland nurseries, fish hatcheries, aquacultural suppliers, government agencies, and conservation groups are dedicated to helping you realize your aquatic ambitions. When I began to study pond design almost 20 years ago, it wasn't that way at all. Ponds were pretty much confined to farms, fish hatcheries, and college lectures on Thoreau. Today the *New York Times* profiles suburbanites enjoying their "liquid lawns" (no mowing necessary), and lily pools have become the hottest trend in landscape gardening. Fly-fishermen build ponds to practice casting. The Environmental Protection Agency (EPA) requires developers to build artificial wetlands to compensate for natural ones disturbed by construction projects. New prairie ponds are credited with helping to restore the population of migrating waterfowl. Fish farming is taking up the slack for losses in ocean fish catches. It's encouraging to think that with a small pond in the yard, you can help to create a wildlife haven as well as a human retreat.

I do a lot of work as an aquacultural consultant checking out potential pond sites, planning water features, and brainstorming remedies for ailing ponds. I've found that people usually need two things (besides more money): basic information about the fundamentals of pond construction and use, and references to regulations, sources of information, and suppliers. *Earth Ponds Sourcebook* provides both. The book is organized into five chapters: Pond Building, Maintenance, Activities and Use, Wildlife, and Garden Ponds. Each chapter concludes with a comprehensive Resources section listing the best references I know in the business. If you're looking for a design approach or maintenance solution and it doesn't appear in the text, you should be able to track down sources for further information in Resources. And if you know of a supplier or technique that I don't, let me know. Suppliers come and go and addresses change, but I'll do my best to keep the guide up to date. Again, reader feedback will be welcome. (Write to *Earth Ponds* editor, The Countryman Press, PO Box 748, Woodstock, Vermont 05091.)

Earth Ponds Sourcebook is designed as a companion to *Earth Ponds: The Country Pond Maker's Guide to Building, Maintenance and Restoration.* Given the huge growth of interest in ponds and aquaculture, a wealth of new materials and suppliers, and new building and maintenance techniques, *Earth Ponds Sourcebook* throws out a larger net, intended to catch the fish I missed before and the new ones that have come along. It is a book that focuses on process and resources, while the original *Earth Ponds* offers in-depth experience and building techniques. It is my intention that the books will complement each other.

However, you can rely only so much on a book to design or improve a pond. Ponds are extraordinarily site specific, which is why you won't find a list of pond contractors in here. Contracting is one of the few commodities that hasn't been mass marketed, so you'll have to track down your own builder. Take your time; it's the most important element in getting a good job done. Look for someone with extensive experience, and check out his references and his ponds. (This may not be necessary in the case of a garden pool, which often can be a successful do-it-yourself project.)

The philosophy behind this book is similar to that underlying the original *Earth Ponds.* Water is a sacred resource. The best-constructed ponds are the most "natural," and each pond ought to be designed to enhance the general environment. During construction, precautions should be taken to minimize damage to the surrounding watershed, care should be taken to make the pond look natural within the contours of the surrounding land, and runoff should be controlled to prevent erosion and downstream siltation. State and federal regulations should be followed. Ask yourself if the planet's ecology will be as good or better off because of the project. If not, why bother?

Before you decide to become a pond owner, there are a few caveats to be aware of. Keeping ponds pristine is fraught with perils, including the use of toxic chemicals to eradicate algae. Gin-clear water belongs in swimming pools, not in ponds. Hence my emphasis on using biological and manual controls. Levees and embankments aren't invulnerable. Recently, a brand-new dam blew out near where I live, flooding the town and killing a fleeing woman. The larger the pond, the greater potential for damage. Building a pond in a wetland may or may not be legal, depending on the area, but it will not be pleasant if the spillway is then plugged up by neighboring beavers. The best argument for staying out of wetlands is practical, not legal. Beware: Faustian bargains abound.

On the other hand, it's possible to look at ponds in a new and more ecologically based way, and, at the same time, avoid some of the problems that come with trying to control natural processes. Why not live in closer harmony with nature? In *Earth Ponds Sourcebook* you'll find a strong focus on wildlife ponds and wetlands. This is a natural evolution of the philosophy of the original *Earth Ponds,* with its emphasis on letting things go their own way. I see the pond keeper's role as one of stewardship rather than absolute control. If you want a swimming pool, okay. Just don't get the two mixed up.

Finally, consider the potential for pond-based planetary healing. We all know that the Earth needs our help, but agreeing on solutions isn't easy. Trash-to-energy garbage incinerators stir up fears of toxic fumes and poisonous ash by-products. Forget alternative fuels until big oil loses its grip on government. High-speed trains scare people off with their fat bottom lines. Naturally, recycling gets the nod, along with a reduced waste stream. Any other low-budget cures? Why not ponds: simple, elegant, small-scale reservoirs of water.

New ponds can be used to replace wetlands lost to development and to create wildlife refuges. Wastewater can be treated, inexpensively and without chemical side effects, in man-made sewage marshes. Fish crops lost to ocean contamination and overfishing can be supplemented by hatcheries and ponds.

Communities threatened by global warming can dig reservoirs for emergency water storage and drought relief. Ponds can be scooped out for nontoxic biological pest control—excavating a mosquito-ridden marsh, for instance—which will then support fish hungry for mosquito larvae, in addition to creating a body of water generally less insect-friendly. Hydropower turbines often feed off a pond used to reserve water and control flow. And, of course, ponds are often dug for agricultural irrigation. These are all proven aquacultural strategies, many of them backed up by centuries of experience.

Aldrich's Pork Barrel

Near my home in central Vermont I can trace the history of aquatic solutions in an old mountain pond: Aldrich's Pork Barrel, it's called, after the neighboring farmer who made it famous more than a century ago. What's interesting about the pond is the way that it has evolved from an ancient beaver impoundment to a source of hydropower and more, providing many overlapping community benefits.

Beavers arrived first, damming a postglacial wetland and creating a feeding area and habitat for other critters, including humans. In fact, in a Native American myth the beaver gets credit for creating Earth itself. The Native Americans understood that it is the inevitable evolution of beaver pond into beaver meadow that produces the fertile terrain necessary to support wild and domesticated foods, as well as game animals.

No artifacts of the Abenaki people, who hunted and fished in this part of Vermont, remain around Aldrich's Pork Barrel, but it's easy to imagine a Native camp there. The cattails and fiddlehead ferns onshore would have appealed to the Abenaki as much as the alders and poplars attracted beavers.

In the mid-18th century, a permanent settlement was established by the pond. A Tory family began farming, drawn to the year-round supply of fish and wildlife. It was the first homestead in the county, and that it happened to be on the shore of a pond was no accident. A sure supply of food, ice, and water was the best household insurance available.

During the Revolutionary War, the Tories were kicked out and a family named Miller took over the farm. They grew flax to produce linen and linseed oil. Flax needs a damp climate to thrive, and plenty of water for fiber processing, and the pond supplied it. The Millers built an overnight station for the stagecoach on the new road from Concord, New Hampshire, to Montpelier, Vermont. Way stations traditionally were built near ponds and lakes so that horses and livestock being transported would have water. Later the pond was dammed to supply power for several mills downstream. Neighboring dairy farmers cut and harvested ice in winter to take care of their refrigeration requirements. Farms around the pond flourished.

Then, in 1816, a series of disastrous frosts destroyed the crops. They called it The Year of Eighteen and Froze to Death, which pretty well describes the fate of many North Country farmers and their animals during the

ensuing winter. But people close to the pond chopped through the ice and caught enough fish to survive. Old man Aldrich found fishing such a pleasant alternative to slopping pigs that he quit farming altogether, and the pond found its name.

A little over a century later, Aldrich's Pork Barrel again provided a remedy for disaster. In 1938 a hurricane flattened woodlots throughout Vermont, and the sawmills couldn't handle the mammoth timber harvest that followed. Much of the wood seemed doomed to rot or to harden beyond the cutting capacity of the mills. So the farmers hitched up their horses and dragged the logs to the pond. Submerged in water, protected from the decaying effect of oxygen, the timber remained moist and resistant to hardening, and the sawmills were able to catch up with the surplus.

Electricity came to the hills in the 1950s. Suddenly every requirement for pond power seemed outdated. Mills once powered by waterwheels switched to electric power. Dairy farmers who had used ice for refrigeration plugged in electric coolers. It wasn't long before many of the farms grew back to brush, abandoned as their owners moved down into the valleys to take advantage of the new economies of scale: Get big or get out.

Yet as Vermont industry turned away from farming, new economic opportunities arose: recreation and conservation. Revenues from fishing licenses and tourist taxes were needed to replace those lost with the mills and farms. The state built a fishing access at the pond and began to stock the water with trout. Together, the town and state set aside a large stretch of the shoreland as a conservation zone. Not long ago the original farm was converted to a summer camp for children, and the echo of a square dance fiddle replaced the screech of waterpowered saw blades. As ever, Aldrich's Pork Barrel offers valuable solutions to community needs.

As we look now for healing solutions for the whole planet, the story of this Vermont pond is worth remembering. We might also recall the advice of Cato the Elder to a declining Roman Empire some 2,000 years ago: "Do they not heap mischief upon mischief: and none for this is to be blamed but ourselves because we do not have our ponds as we ought to have about our house."

EARTH PONDS *Sourcebook*

Give a man a fish and you feed him for a day. Teach a man how to fish and you feed him for a lifetime.

—Chinese proverb

ᔕ

It's a poor frog that won't holler for its own pond.

—Vermont proverb

22-B

1. POND BUILDING

There seems to be something downright arcane about pond building, as if success depends on a combination of good luck, perfect weather, and the proper alignment of the stars. Introduce a couple of pond owners and they'll soon be trading tales of sunken bulldozers and leaky spillways. But beneath the mystique, there's a blueprint successful pond makers adhere to, and a sequence of steps likely to lead to success.

Siting

To build or not to build is the most important decision you'll make. Choosing the pond site boils down to finding plentiful clean water and low-infiltration soils in an area you'd enjoy adding a pond to, as well as complying with building regulations, if any. A pond that continually overflows is healthiest, which usually means finding a location where on-site springs are vigorous enough to supplement low-watershed runoff during dry, hot summer months. Good water sources usually include a combination of on-site groundwater (spring fed or water table) and intermittent watershed runoff. Sometimes a stream can be used to feed a pond, but you'll have to take care not to allow erosion to fill the pond with silt. Streams and brooks can also be used to feed a pond through a gravity bypass pipe system, which will help prevent siltation. Pumps and hydraulic rams can be used to deliver water, but you should weigh seriously the complications and expense before committing to mechanical water-delivery systems. One of the great charms of a successful pond is its self-sufficiency, which is considerably reduced when artificial water-support systems are involved.

There's nothing backward about using a backhoe to help you zero in on a suitable pond site. In short order and without any backstrain, backhoe test borings reveal soil composition, water table, and ledge obstructions. Be sure to refill the holes if there's any potential danger to children or animals. If you leave the test pits open, don't allow excavated material to sit too close to the edge; it may wash back in or cause the pit to slump.

Finding water is usually a matter of direct observation. Soggy sags that stay wet through the summer often make good sites, as do areas that support water-loving vegetation. It's often easy for me to disqualify a site if the ground cover shows no evidence of promising plants, such as ferns, alder, or even a blanket of lush grass. Parched, stunted grass in dusty soil is not an auspicious vision. You might be surprised how many people call me in to evaluate such an area. I usually tell them to build a swimming pool.

If you've lived on a piece of land long enough, you should have a rough idea of where the water hangs out,

Several test borings have been dug here, and the pond site is being staked and measured.

especially during the dry summer weeks. In hill country you're most likely to wind up putting your pond in a low-lying area. Why? The lower you go, the more reliable your water. In a pinch, you might call in a dowser to help locate a site.

After you've chosen one or more potential pond sites, it's time to confirm them. Most questions about site qualifications will be answered by digging a few test pits. Three or four 8- to 10-foot-deep holes, throughout the site, are usually dug by backhoe to reveal water table, soil composition, and presence of ledge. Test borings are most reliable if dug during dry weather. The soil should contain enough clay to hold together in a ball when compressed in your hand. Beware of sand and shale, which can cause leakage. Also, beware of ledge, which can obstruct excavation and drain water. Smaller test pits can be drilled using a hand auger. If you have a wetland that you're considering making into a pond, be aware of potential beaver problems. Unless you intend to support a beaver population, you may be asking for trouble (see Beaver Management, pages 126–32).

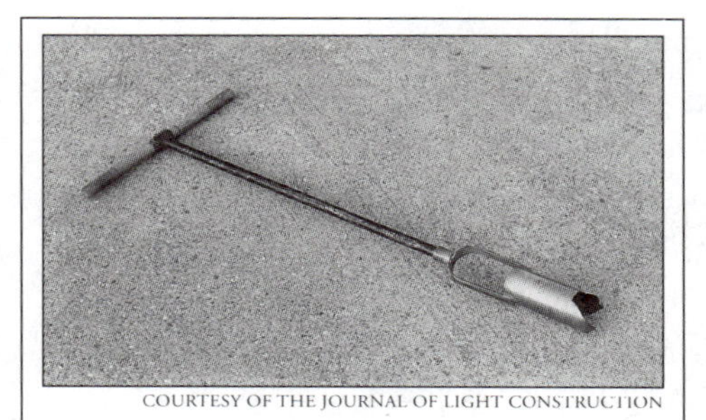

COURTESY OF THE JOURNAL OF LIGHT CONSTRUCTION

Use a hand auger for preliminary soil tests. There are two types: a pigtail auger, which has a spiral bit like a ship's auger; and a bucket auger, shown here. Both types are available with threaded extensions for probing deep below the surface. Hand augers can be used to sample soil composition and reveal water table, although they're less definitive about finding ledge. They're especially useful in remote areas and whenever hiring a backhoe isn't economical.

The soil should include roughly 10 to 20 percent clay, with a minimum of sand, gravel, and shale. An earth pond will lose some water through natural seepage and evaporation, but ideally the water level will not fluctuate dramatically. Soils subject to a high degree of infiltration (leaky, that is) can be remedied with various amendments including clay, bentonite, and polymer compounds, as well as with a physical barrier made of plastic or rubber. Clay is the traditional solution to porous soil, usually trucked in to the pond site when insufficient amounts of it are naturally present. If you're lucky you'll find clay nearby, perhaps even at another location on your land. Otherwise, the cost of long-distance trucking may be prohibitive. On some projects I've worked on, fill from the pond excavation was traded for imported clay. When clay is impractical, bentonite is often used. Bentonite is a colloidal clay mined mostly in the West and shipped in dry form. With the addition of water, it swells as much as 20 times in size, and makes an effective liner when correctly applied. It is also available embedded in mats, which are unrolled to create pond-bed water barriers. A polymer emulsion can be applied in liquid form for dry or for full ponds. It has the consistency of a gritty white vegetable oil and binds to soil particles, reducing seepage rates as much as 90 percent, according to one manufacturer. Synthetic membranes, usually PVC, can also be used to leakproof a pond. Careful preparation is required to create a smooth pond bed that will not puncture the liner, and special sealing procedures are necessary to bind rolls together. In general, I consider using sealants and liners a last resort and suggest avoiding them if possible. It's better to find a site that won't require such heroic measures.

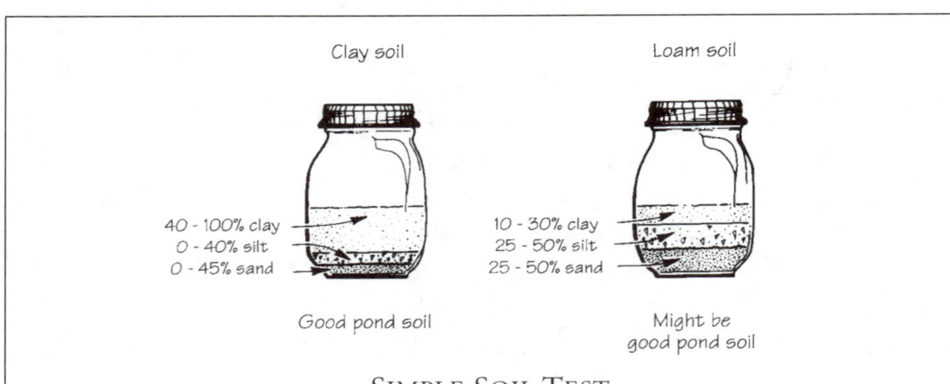

SIMPLE SOIL TEST

To measure the proportion of sand, silt, and clay in a soil sample, place the sample in a glass jar, top it off with water, and cap the jar. Then shake it and let settle for 24 hours. For good pond soil, the top stratum of clay should comprise at least 20 percent of the total volume of soil in the jar.

COURTESY OF THE JOURNAL OF LIGHT CONSTRUCTION

Your pond site will also determine the building style. On flat terrain where no embankments are required, ponds are excavated. Although some earth removed from an excavated pond will be used to build a well-drained surrounding terrace, most material will have to be removed; it may be used for nearby landscaping or fill. On sloping land an embankment may be needed to complete the basin. Embankments are often built with the earth removed during excavation, and no further trucking is needed. Most experienced contractors prefer to build embankments with soil that's had time to dry out, making it easier to shape and compact. Compacting the soil that lines the pond is essential if it is to successfully hold water.

Design Features

Once you've zeroed in on one or more promising sites, it's time to consider how you plan to use the pond. Form follows function in aquaculture as well as architecture, and most aspects of pond building—site, size, and budget—are determined by its intended applications. Today most large ponds are built for multiple use: swimming, landscaping, and perhaps raising fish. In the North, skating is another plus. Often a multipurpose recreational pond can be used to irrigate a garden and even supply household water during a drought. Other potential uses include wildlife support, livestock watering, fire protection, and even hydropower. Sometimes people simply want a pond that is attractive to look at. Some functions may be mutually exclusive. A pond used for irrigation or livestock may not be suitable for swimming or raising fish. Determining your priorities will help you design your pond.

Perhaps you're interested in developing an independent source of hydropowered electricity. Ponds used for hydropower usually require a constant overflow to power the turbine. Ponds for water gardening will benefit from shelves installed just below the waterline for bog plants. If you plan to use a pond to water livestock, consider strategic fencing to direct animals to a specific area; otherwise you open all the banks to erosion. Fencing may also be

Left: *This drop inlet with drain will handle overflow as well as provide a means to empty the pond for repairs, cleanouts, and fish harvests. Drains are usually located well away from inflows to prevent silt from burying the pipe. Piping systems should be fitted with antiseep collars to prevent leaks.* Below: *Earth-cut spillways are commonly found in excavated ponds or embankment ponds when the overflow channel can be protected against erosion. This earth-cut spillway features a fence to keep in the fish.*

necessary for suburban ponds, where safety or insurance regulations require such protection. Ponds for wildlife are most effective when sited at some distance from human activity, to encourage animal attraction. Fire protection ponds should be located where a fire truck has year-round access; in the North Country this usually means near a plowed road. These ponds often have a dry hydrant installed during construction. Ponds for cold-water fish will usually be dug deeper than those for warm-, and in general fishponds in the North should be at least 8 feet deep to help prevent winterkill. Naturally enough, you won't want a pond for skinny-dipping to be located alongside Main Street. Wetland ponds will often incorporate shallow zones to encourage plant growth and "speed bumps" to keep silt from slumping into deeper areas. Ponds that feature a swimming area may incorporate a shallow slope for water access; during construction this area is often excavated and filled with washed sand. Finally, ponds used for commercial fish culture usually incorporate drains for cleaning and harvest.

The point of this quick survey of design features is to alert you to the large spectrum of options your pond offers and to prompt you to focus on the ones that will be your top priority. You'll want to make sure that they will function together. For example, if you build a pond for livestock watering and later decide you'd like to use it for swimming, there may be a long, drawn-out cleanout involved. With ponds—as with other things—it's tough to change horses in midstream. Think ahead. Let your contractor know how you plan to use the pond and work with him on developing the design. For example, it's usually more economical to do all the piping during initial construction than to tear up the pond a few years down the road for add-ons. And be sure to check out neighborhood ponds for design ideas and potential features. Don't forget to ask about mistakes other pond owners might have made. Pond building is as much an art as it is a science, and you can learn as much in the field as you can in any book, including this one.

Watershed Reckoning

Your pond will be affected by the size and ground cover of the watershed draining into the site. In general, the bigger the watershed, the bigger the pond potential. (Of course, too much water can pose its own problems.) The slope of the land and your average regional rainfall will also have bearing on the volume of water available. The US Department of Agriculture (USDA) publishes a pond design booklet that includes data for calculating pond size according to watershed (Handbook 590, *Ponds—Planning, Design, Construction;* see Resources, page 38). This booklet, along with helpful maps and information, is available from your local Natural Resources Conservation Service (NRCS) office.

The watershed is the total land area that will eventually drain into your pond. Every square foot of land that funnels precipitation and groundwater to the pond site affects the volume and water quality of the reservoir. When you know the watershed acreage, you can calculate pond capacity.

To figure your watershed, use NRCS maps and photographs, or a US Geological Survey topographical map (see Resources, page 39). If you're not familiar with the technique of reading a topo map, you'll be better off taking advantage of the Natural Resources Conservation Service; the folks there can calculate acreage for you. Otherwise, trace the contours of the area that drains into the site. You're looking for ridgelines, which indicate where runoff will break toward your site. It also helps to walk the land to determine the size of the area that feeds the site. Once you've walked the land, you should be able to imagine roughly how the watershed lies and to locate the corresponding contours on the map. Using the map's scale, draw a grid over the watershed area so that each square in the grid equals 1 acre (approximately 209 feet square). Count the number of squares (estimate the area of partial squares) to get the total acreage of the watershed.

Pond Physique

The topography of the site and its setting usually suggest how large and what shape the pond should be. When you know the total number of acres that shed water into your pond site, you can match the storage capacity of the pond to the water supply.

The water storage volume of a pond is usually counted in acre-feet. To calculate acre-footage, first determine the surface area of the pond. For a nearly round pond, this is a matter of simple geometry: Area = πr^2. For an irregularly shaped pond, plot the shore-

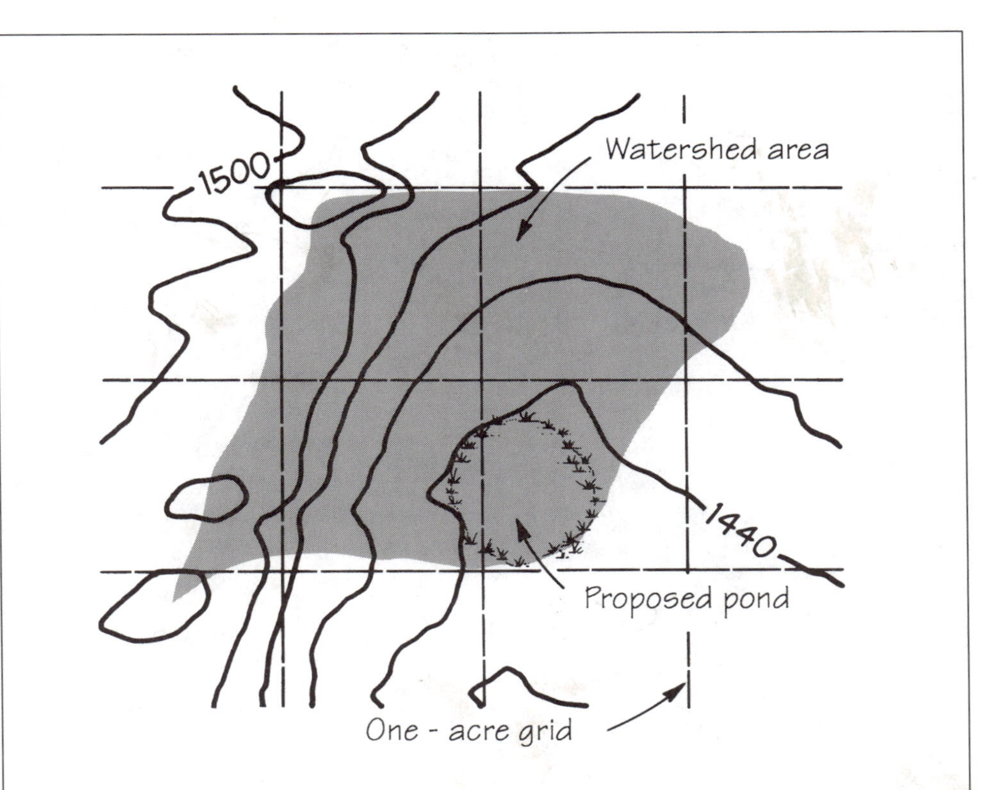

CALCULATING WATERSHED AREA

To determine the watershed area for a pond, trace the contours of the area that drains into the pond site on a topographical map. Using the map's scale, superimpose a grid of 1-acre squares, then count the number of squares in the watershed area to calculate its total acreage. The watershed area in the illustration (shown in gray) comprises about 3¼ acres.

COURTESY OF THE JOURNAL OF LIGHT CONSTRUCTION

line to a convenient scale on graph paper and figure the area as you did for determining watershed area, by counting the squares (1 acre = 43,560 square feet).

Next, estimate the depth. The acre-footage formula averages the depth of all ponds at a uniform 40 percent of maximum, so multiply the desired maximum water depth by 0.4. Take the result and multiply it by the surface area to get acre-footage, or pond capacity. For example, the pond shown in the illustration on page 25 is estimated to be 17,671 square feet. To calculate its capacity, refer to the sidebar.

> **HOW TO CALCULATE POND CAPACITY**
>
> *Pond Surface Area*
>
> 17,671 sq. ft. ÷ 43,560 sq. ft. per acre = 0.41 acre
>
> *Average Pond Depth*
>
> 10 ft. max. depth × 0.4 (40% of max.) = 4 ft.
>
> *Pond Capacity*
>
> 4 ft. × 0.41 acres = 1.64 acre-ft.

The final step is to adjust the size of the pond to its watershed. In prime pond-making country east of the Mississippi and in the Northwest, this rule of thumb determines the ratio of watershed acreage to pond capacity: Each acre-foot of pond should receive runoff from territory no larger than 2 acres, if the ground cover is all woods or brush. If the ground cover is pasture, the drainage area should not exceed 1½ acres for each acre-foot of pond. On cultivated land, each acre-foot should receive runoff from no more than 1 acre. If the watershed is mixed, calculate accordingly. The pond on page 25, which is located in a wooded area, can hold all of the water that drains from about 3¼ acres (1.64 acre-feet × 2) and so is well matched to its watershed area.

Spillways

Knowing your watershed size will also help you to determine spillway design. The *spillway* is the pipe, stream, or overflow gate that channels water as it leaves the pond. The bigger the watershed, the bigger and/or tougher the spillway must be. When that 50-year-frequency storm comes around, you'll want a spillway big enough to transport the overflow back to the original stream that carried away watershed runoff before the pond was built. And you'll want it to be tough enough to withstand the eroding forces of that overflow. Piped spillways can be drop inlets, with or without a drain, usually found in embankment ponds; horizontal, culvert-style pipes at surface level; reinforced earthen spillways; and wood or concrete gates (usually adjustable to regulate water level), which create a waterfall exiting the pond.

Each of these spillways has its own design requirements. Pipe needs to be carefully sized to match the watershed, exposed overflows should be reinforced against erosion, and gates must include erosion-proof wings. "Emergency" spillways are often included in the pond design to carry off excess overflow during worst-case storm scenarios. Emergency spillways are usually grassy channels set at a level somewhere between the primary spillway and the rim of the embankment or shore around the pond. The smaller the watershed, the better the chance to use a surface spillway reinforced with stone or riprap. It saves on materials and installation costs, and it can never rust.

Earth spillways make the most sense for excavated ponds, where you're unlikely to install a drain anyway, and where horizontal surface level pipes are often vulnerable to leaks. But they can be used in embankment ponds, also, as long as the watershed isn't so large that it's likely to cause erosion in the spillway channel. Earth spillways can also be landscaped to create an attractive stream. You might want to take a look at neighboring ponds for ideas about spillway design, but don't forget to inquire about their watershed size. Refer also to USDA Handbook 590 for more details. I also recommend a talk with your county NRCS agent to help you determine spillway design and materials.

This drop inlet may not leak, but it's vulnerable on two other levels: Without a protective trash guard or screen, it could become clogged with leaves and debris; and sitting in deep water makes it susceptible to ice damage. Drop inlets closer to shore benefit from being reinforced by the surrounding earth.

Choosing a Contractor

During your site search it may be helpful to enlist the aid of a contractor or consultant. In fact, considering the myriad ways in which a pond project can go astray, the sooner you get a contractor or consultant involved, the better. (Unless, of course, you've had sufficient experience in landscaping and/or contracting projects to give you the confidence to supervise the project on your own.) Ask your neighbors about recent pond projects in the area and who built them. Your town clerk may also have leads about nearby projects. The NRCS or your local extension service may be able to provide names of contractors.

Obviously, you're looking for a contractor with a good track record. If he can show you a half-dozen ponds or so that turned out well for their owners, and his price is reasonable, you're in luck. You can probably pick up some design ideas from visiting other ponds, too. You will also want to ask about contracts and guarantees. Some builders will give you a contract price for the whole job; others prefer to be paid for time and materials. Depending on the project, either arrangement can be acceptable. I tend to prefer a contract price so that the owner doesn't wind up paying for downtime lost to bad weather or other unforeseen slowdowns. On the other hand, I know one pond builder who works for time and materials only, because, as he says, "every project winds up different from the way it was planned." The pond may get bigger, require different features, or need additional materials. Either way, you want somebody who agrees to make the work good if something goes wrong—if the pond doesn't fill up, for instance.

A friend of mine asked whether it's possible for an amateur to build and maintain a pond by depending on experts. The only reasonable answer is that it depends on the experts. It always comes down to putting the right guy in the bulldozer seat. Naturally, in order to make that choice and be able to discuss options intelligently, the more you know, the better off you'll be. Read a few books, check out local ponds, take advantage of your NRCS and extension service, hire a consultant (if you can find one; pond building isn't yet as popular as mutual fund investments), and ask several contractors to come in and give you their opinion on potential sites (you'll get a variety of suggestions, as well as bids). Landscape contractors can be another good source of information and possible design work.

Before construction begins, the site should be cleared of trees and shrubs. Topsoil is usually stripped and stockpiled for later use in landscaping. A bulldozer makes quick work of shrub removal, although you may find that doing it yourself results in less debris.

Be clear about what you expect the contractor to do. If you're building an excavated pond, will the contractor be responsible for removing all material? Are you going to save money by raking, seeding, and mulching around the pond, or will that be done by your contractor? When will the entire project be finished?

Budget estimates vary according to local contracting rates, but in general a pond will cost between $1 and $5 per cubic yard of volume. To determine yardage, calculate the volume of the basin and divide by 27. For example, a pond that's roughly 100 feet square by 8 feet deep has a volume of 80,000 cubic feet. Divide by 27: That's 2,963 cubic yards, or roughly between $3,000 and $15,000. Piping costs may add to this figure.

Permits

Before beginning construction, be sure you have complied with building regulations and conservation laws. The best pond sites often turn up in areas that are protected by wetland regulations. Your municipal clerk should be able to tell you if a pond needs a local permit, and perhaps additional permitting from the state and/or federal government. Your NRCS, Extension Service, and state Department of Natural Resources can help clarify permitting obligations. Also, be sure your land title is clear, without restrictions or easements. Double-check that no underground piping or electric lines run through the area. Overhead electric lines also can pose a hazard.

Construction

Once you've selected a site, obtained any necessary permits, and found a contractor, it's time to clear the area. If the site is not wooded, you're a step ahead of the game. But brush and trees will have to be removed, either by you or by your contractor. If the site is covered with only small brush and trees, it may be possible for the contractor to skim it clear rapidly with a bulldozer. If you decide on this approach, plan for disposal of the debris. In most cases it should not be buried in the structure of the pond, particularly a water-retaining embankment. This organic material will eventually decay and could lead to sinkholes, depressions, and, worst of all, leaks. I've been called in on more than one leaky pond where the problem turned out to have been built into the project during construction: tree trunks buried in the dam. Near some sites it's not difficult to find a location to pile up wooded debris where it eventually can be burned or—even better—allowed to compost. If you have trouble finding such a place, consider using a chipper to mulch the material. This is something you may want to do yourself, with a rented chipper, or you can leave it up to your contractor. Beware, though: Chippers are dangerous and require protective clothing and eyewear.

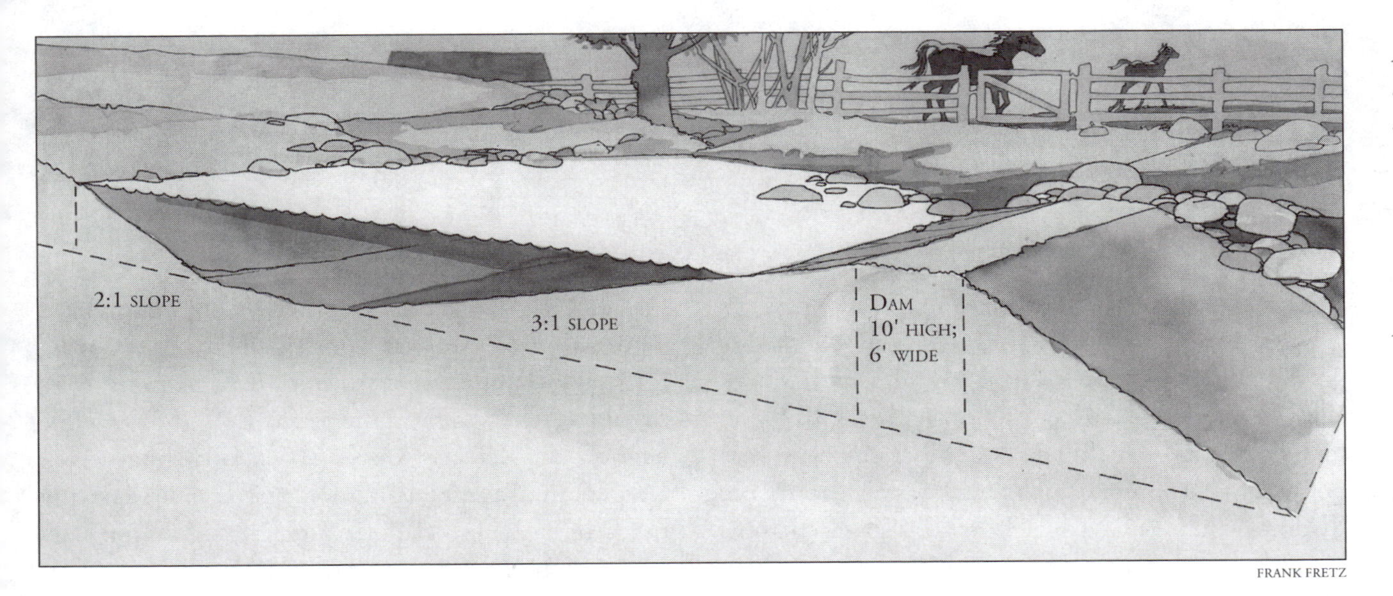

FRANK FRETZ

Although a steep bank (left) discourages weed growth, slopes steeper than 2:1 (horizontal to vertical) may cave in. A shallow bank (right) can serve as a beach or boat ramp. The dam must be wide and shallow to prevent erosion.

Less is not more when it comes to building a dam. This hefty embankment was built by using material excavated from the pond basin—creating a solid retaining wall to protect against washouts as well as utilizing the material dug out of the site to deepen the pond.

If your back is up to it and you've got some skills with a chain saw, there are several advantages to clearing a wooded site yourself. You'll save money by cutting down on your contractor's time. By going at it gradually, you may be able to harvest firewood or other useful material from the site that would otherwise be uneconomical for the contractor to separate, stack, and so on. By doing the clearing yourself, you'll also get to know the pond site and perhaps be more appreciative of surrounding features that might enhance the pond. Imagine cutting a tree that could otherwise have supported a tree swing over the water or shaded the beach during the peak of summer. For the most part, however, trees should be removed from the perimeter, although some landowners prefer a wooded shore for habitat cover. Keep in mind that higher water levels could kill nearby trees, and that leaf deposits nourish algae. You may want to wait until the pond fills before making a deci-

As a house rises on the hill above, this new pond is also rising. On the opposite shore, stones selected from the excavation have been positioned to create diving rocks when the pond is full. Spec contractors often build ponds in tandem with home construction to enhance sales appeal.

sion about some nearby trees. Who knows, during the clearing process you may even discover a good reason or two *not* to build a pond there. That kind of about-face is much more difficult to make after the diesel engines have started roaring.

If you are clearing a wooded site yourself, be sure to leave 3- to 4-foot stumps on trees over 6 inches in diameter to give the bulldozer operator leverage when uprooting the stumps. If the site is going to be worked by a rubber-tire backhoe, be careful not to leave sharp stumps at ground level; they can flatten tires.

The best time for construction is during dry weather, to minimize difficulties (and expenses) with bogged-down equipment. Drying out the site is often accelerated by digging a drainage ditch through the area well before construction begins. Once construction is under way, remind your contractor to reserve the initial shavings of topsoil for use later in landscaping.

ANATOMY OF A DAM

1. Dam construction begins with the removal of topsoil throughout the foundation area and the creation of a core trench. The core trench should be deep enough to get below sand to clay or bedrock; the sides can be slanted or vertical. If your best clay material is in short supply, be sure to use it on the front half of the dam.

2. Material around pipe spillways should be thoroughly compacted to eliminate air pockets. Antiseep collars are also essential to prevent leaks. The drop inlet should be located close to the shore to take advantage of the earth reinforcement, which is especially helpful against ice damage. If you include a drain, reduce the size of the spillway pipe to prevent downstream erosion during drawdowns. Be sure the drain intake is high enough above the pond bed to prevent burial in silt. Most ponds incorporating piped spillways also feature a secondary or emergency spillway to carry away floodwater that exceeds pipe capacity during unusually heavy runoff periods. The emergency spillway is usually an earth-cut channel 1 to 1½ feet above the principal spillway inlet, with the top of the dam another foot or so higher still.

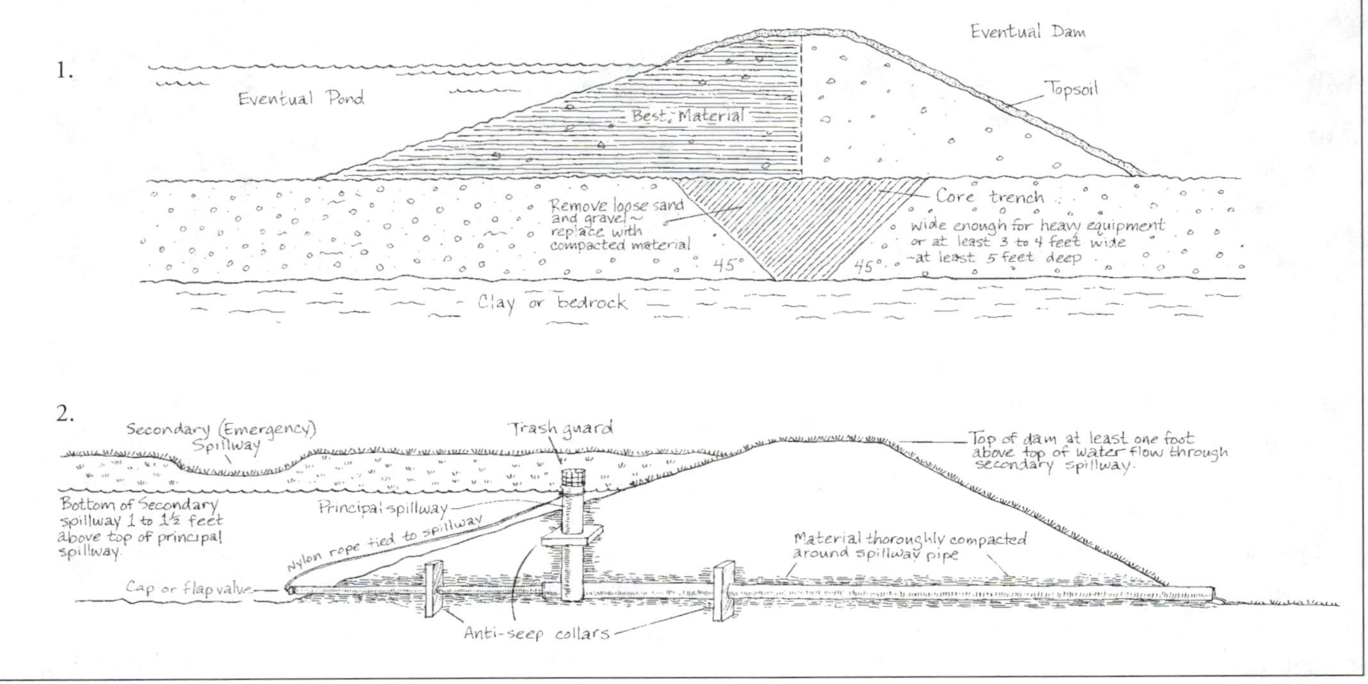

DRAWINGS BY ELAYNE SEARS

As I mentioned earlier, the pond site will determine the building style. Flat terrain calls for excavated ponds; sloping land demands some kind of embankment. Don't forget to make provisions for dispersal of any excavated material not used in a dam or in terracing around the pond.

Pond basin slopes should be cut at a 3:1 angle to discourage weeds and algae. One exception to this is a beach area, where shallow-water vegetation will be discouraged by the mulching effect of sand. Unpiped inflows and outflows should be lined with riprap (industrial crushed rock) or fieldstone to prevent erosion. Where the terrain permits, designers sometimes site exposed spillways in a shoreline area featuring ledge or other large stone features, to take advantage of the natural reinforcement. Thus, costly overflow piping may not be necessary if a sturdy natural spillway feature can be taken advantage of.

Piping can be a worthwhile investment, though, especially in embankment ponds. Properly installed drop outlets overcome potential problems with overflow erosion, and when combined with a drain enable the pond owner to lower the water level for fish harvests, cleaning, and repairs. Pipe must be correctly sized and installed. Heavy rains can overwhelm undersized pipe outlets, leading to embankment failure. Improperly collared pipes are susceptible to erosion around the exterior of the outlet. Be sure your inlet pipe diameter corresponds to NRCS recommendations, and that your contractor is not a novice at pond plumbing.

The topsoil you saved at the beginning of construction can now be spread out on the shore as a seedbed for grass. Final landscaping is usually delayed until the shore area dries out. I don't recommend fertilizing the nearby shoreland because high nutrient runoff is likely to trigger the growth of algae and aquatic weeds.

Your new pond may need a year or so to season. Turbid water can be slow to clear, and water levels often remain low until the soil "heals." But if you've done your homework, one day you should be able to look out over a pond that any self-respecting beaver would be proud to call home—and, one day, just might.

The word pond was once synonymous with farm pond. Farmers were among the earliest pond designers and builders, and small reservoirs guaranteed water for crops, livestock, raising fish, and fire protection, and ice for refrigeration.

Pooling Your Resources

Hank is a neighbor of mine. He's a truck farmer growing vegetables and grain, and he wants to increase his acreage. That means extra irrigation. A pond would do the trick. Because he lives on a sidehill out beyond the electric line, he also wants waterpower to drive a hydro generator. A pond would put him in the 20th century. Ten years ago I helped Hank work on pond site selection. But it wasn't until this past August that excavation began. Why the holdup? To build his 1-acre reservoir, Hank needed about $6,000, and that was way over his head. Then, last year, some friends nearby offered to contribute if they could use the pond for swimming, sauna baths, and skating. Construction is now under way, and Hank is plowing new fields. Coming up: irrigation and hydropower for the farm, and a beach for his neighbors.

Cooperative pond building is appropriate aquaculture. It's not a new idea; people have been digging ponds communally for centuries. But now it involves a new blend of pond makers, community interests, and technique. For instance, an irrigation pond that drops 3 or 4 feet in August to quench the crops won't appeal much to swimmers. Nor will it turn an electric turbine. That's why Hank and his partners are excavating in a rich watershed to maximize overflow. Hefty ponds with cascades of surplus water can fulfill more roles than can little ones.

There's plenty of room for microponds, too. In fact, while the number of our country's farms dwindles in inverse proportion to their acreage, the reverse is true in aquaculture. More ponds are being dug now than ever before, and they're getting smaller. The same technology that gives us microchips and ultralight aircraft enables pond makers to reduce their reservoirs to the size of a washtub. Often it's being done with synthetic basin materials and mechanical aeration systems. But pond makers are also taking advantage of traditional small-scale, low-cost Asian and East European aquacultural methods, newly introduced to these shores. These involve using earth-bottomed ponds, which can provide natural feed for fish and other aquacultural crops; pond rotation to allow habitats to lie fallow, eliminate weeds, and regenerate nutrients; and polyculture of waterfowl and fish together in one pond, whereby waterfowl waste nourishes aquatic growth, which in turn nourishes the fish.

Once upon a time the US Department of Agriculture and the Natural Resources Conservation Service helped fund pond makers, but those good old days are fading. Pond-making co-ops offer a way to take up the slack. And partnerships need not be confined to farming. Ponds often turn up when a landowner teams up with his town. Our local village athletic organization helped gather donations to build a recreation pond. Other pond partnerships involve fishing clubs, land trusts, real-estate developments, and fire departments.

One innovative team emerged recently in Wells, Maine. The townspeople were plagued by mosquitoes. Nobody wanted to spray with pesticides. So one family dug a pond and the town put up $1,000 to stock it with dragonflies, which are big mosquito-guzzlers. Now the mosquitoes get eaten, not the people. And there's a new pond on the planet. The rest of us benefit indirectly from the creation of a wildlife feeding station and wetland. *That's* pooling your resources.

PRODUCTS & SUPPLIERS

Water Delivery Systems

These companies sell pumps, non-electric waterpowered rams, and wind-powered water pumps and aerators. Call or write for a catalog.

Aquacenter, Inc.
166 Seven Oaks Road
Leland, MS 38756
1-800-748-8921

Aquatic Eco-Systems, Inc.
1767 Benbow Court
Apopka, FL 32703
1-800-422-3939

D & L Wholesale, Inc.
PO Box 1309
149 South Boulevard
Clinton, NC 28328
1-800-334-8912

Deep Rock Manufacturing Co.
2200 Anderson Road
PO Box 1
Opelika, AL 36803-0001
1-800-633-8774

Manufactures the do-it-yourself Hydra Drill, a portable one-man well digger.

Eagar, Inc.
PO Box 540476
North Salt Lake, UT 84054
1-800-423-6249

Lehman's
Box 41
Kidron, OH 44636
330-857-5441

Malibu Water Resources
PO Box 134
Malibu, CA 90265
310-317-1624

O'Brock Windmills
North Benton, OH 44449
330-584-4681

Stoney Creek Equipment Co.
11073 Peach Avenue
Grant, MI 49327
1-800-448-3873

Liners

These companies sell various kinds of artificial liners. Call or write for a catalog.

Aquacenter, Inc.
166 Seven Oaks Road
Leland, MS 38756
1-800-748-8921

Aquatic Eco-Systems, Inc.
1767 Benbow Court
Apopka, FL 32703
1-800-422-3939

DLM Plastics
1530 Harvard Avenue
Findlay, OH 45840
1-800-444-5877

DripWorks
231 East San Francisco Street
Willits, CA 95490
1-800-522-3747

Poly-Flex
2000 West Marshall Drive
Grand Prairie, TX 75051
1-800-527-3322

Reef Industries, Inc.
PO Box 750245
Houston, TX 77275-0245
1-800-231-2417

Resource Conservation
Technology, Inc.
2633 North Calvert Street
Baltimore, MD 21218
410-366-1146

Yunker Plastics
PO Box 190
Lake Geneva, WI 53147
1-800-236-3328

Piping

Agri Drain Corporation
PO Box 458
1462 340th Street
Adair, IA 50002
1-800-232-4742

Pond Dam Piping, Ltd.
398 Eighth Street
Macon, GA 31201
1-800-333-2611

Erosion-Control Blankets and Mats

These companies sell various soil protection reinforcements.

Belton Industries, Inc.
8613 Roswell Road
Atlanta, GA 30350
404-587-0257

Bestmann Green Systems, Inc.
53 Mason Street
Salem, MA 01970
508-741-1166

Bon Terra
355 West Chestnut Street
Genesee, ID 83832
1-800-882-9489

Indian Valley Industries, Inc.
PO Box 810
Johnson City, NY 13790
1-800-659-5111

T.C. Mirafi
3500 Parkway Lane, Suite 500
Norcross, GA 30092
1-800-234-0484

RoLanka International, Inc.
6476 Mill Court
Morrow, GA
1-800-760-3215

Verdyol Alabama, Inc.
407 Miles Parkway
PO Box 605
Pell City, AL 35125
205-338-4411

Weyerhaeuser Company
Engineered Fiber Products
CCB 5D6
Tacoma, WA 98477
1-800-704-2278

Soil Sealants

These companies sell soil amendments to help seal leaky ponds.

CETCO
521 East Epsom Road, Unit 1-B
Towson, MD 21286
410-339-7424
Sells bentonite in granular form and as mat liners.

Seepage Control, Inc.
PO Box 51177
Phoenix, AZ 85076-1177
1-800-214-9640

Sells ESS-13, a resinous polymer emulsion used to seal pond beds.

Biological Pest Management

Berkshire Biological
264 Main Road
Westhampton, MA 01027
413-527-3932

Sells dragonfly larvae, which are used for nontoxic mosquito control.

The Green Spot
93 Priest Road
Nottingham, NH 03290
603-942-8925

Sells mosquito dunks (a nontoxic bacterial agent) and bat houses for mosquito control.

Michael Morrison
PO Box 316
York, ME 03909
207-363-2886

Sells mosquito-devouring minnows (mummichogs) and mosquito dunks; works with communities on mosquito control.

Water and Soil Test Kits; pH Test Kits

Aquatic Eco-Systems, Inc.
1767 Benbow Court
Apopka, FL 32703
1-800-422-3939

Hach Company
PO Box 389
Loveland, CO 80539
1-800-227-4224

BOOKS & OTHER PUBLICATIONS

National Wildlife Federation Conservation Directory
National Wildlife Federation
1400 16th Street, NW
Washington, DC 20036-2266
202-797-6800

Aquaculture Magazine
PO Box 2329
Asheville, NC 28802
704-254-7334

Build a Pond for Food and Fun
by D.J. Young
Bulletin A-19
Storey Communications
Schoolhouse Road
Pownal, VT 05261
1-800-441-5700

Building a Pond
Farmer's Bulletin No. 2256
US Department of Agriculture
US Government Printing Office
Washington, DC 20402
202-512-0132

Cottage Water Systems
by Max Burns
Cottage Life Books
11 Queen Street East
Suite 408
Toronto, Ontario M5C 1S2
Canada
416-599-2000

Excellent introduction to pumps and water delivery systems.

Earth Ponds: The Country Pond Maker's Guide to Building, Maintenance and Restoration
by Tim Matson
The Countryman Press
PO Box 748
Woodstock, VT 05091
1-800-233-4830

Tim Matson's Earth Ponds Video
Earth Ponds Co.
288 Miller Pond Road
Thetford Center, VT 05075
802-333-9019

Farm Pond Harvest Magazine
1390 North 14500 E Road
Momence, IL 60954
815-472-2686

Land and Water Magazine
PO Box 1197
Fort Dodge, IA 50501-9925
515-576-3191

Good source of pond designers and builders.

Ponds: Building, Maintaining, and Enjoying
Carolyn Garrick Stern
Progressive Farmer, Inc.
2100 Lakeshore Drive
Birmingham, AL 35209
205-877-6413

A succinct guide to pond construction, management, and use. Recommended.

Ponds—Planning, Design, Construction
Handbook 590
US Department of Agriculture
National Resources
Conservation Service
US Government Printing Office
Washington, DC 20402
202-512-0132

Try your local NRCS office for a copy; otherwise order from the GPO.

The Home Water Supply: How to Find, Filter, Store, and Conserve It
by Stu Campbell
Storey Communications
Schoolhouse Road
Pownal, VT 05261
1-800-441-5700

Excellent survey of household water systems, including a section on ponds.

The Real Goods Solar Living Source Book
by John Schaeffer and Staff
Distributed by Chelsea Green Publishing Co.
PO Box 428
White River Junction, VT 05001
1-800-762-7325

Good section on water and water delivery systems, and sources for equipment.

Waterhole: A Guide to Digging Your Own Well
by Bob Mellin
Balboa Publishing
11 Library Place
San Anselmo, CA 94960
415-453-8886

Topographic Maps

US Geological Survey
Department of the Interior
National Center
Reston, VA 22029
703-648-4000

GOVERNMENT ORGANIZATIONS

Contact your state Natural Resources Board and/or University Extension Service for information regarding pond permitting and construction. An excellent source of addresses for federal and state agencies is the annual *National Wildlife Federation Conservation Directory,* which also lists private organizations concerned with natural resource use and management. The directory includes Canadian federal and provincial agencies and organizations as well (see Books and Other Publications, page 37).

US Department of Agriculture
National Resources Conservation Service
14th and Independence Avenue, SW
PO Box 2890
Washington, DC 20013
202-720-3210

Despite reductions in funding for design support, the NRCS (a new branch of the Soil Conservation Service) can be an excellent source of information regarding pond design, watershed calculation, and spillway requirements. Check your local telephone book for the NRCS office in your county.

US Department of Agriculture
Consolidated Farm Services Agency
PO Box 2415
Washington, DC 20013
202-720-6221

Another newly designated branch of the Soil Conservation Service, the CFSA administers many water programs, and may provide financial support for agricultural water projects, depending on county priorities.

US Army Corps of Engineers
Office of Environmental Policy
20 Massachusetts Avenue, NW
Washington, DC 20314-1000
202-761-0166

The US Army Corps of Engineers has regulatory power over some waterway alteration work, which may include pond building, especially large projects. To find out, contact your local US Army Engineers district office.

US Fish and Wildlife Service
Refuges and Wildlife
4401 N. Fairfax Drive
Arlington, VA 22203
703-358-2161

The Fish and Wildlife Service may be able to provide assistance with wildlife pond design (see Wildlife, page 113). Also ask your state fish and wildlife department for help.

MISCELLANEOUS

Forestry Suppliers, Inc.
PO Box 8397
Jackson, MS 39284-8397
1-800-647-5368

Sells many tools used in pond siting, including hand augers, levels, and map measurement devices. Excellent catalog.

Dowsing

American Society of Dowsers
PO Box 24
Danville, VT 05828
802-684-3417

Books and information about dowsing for water sources and leaks.

2. MAINTENANCE

Whether you build a pond or buy one, the day will come when you're going to have to think about maintenance. It could happen the first year, when the spillway needs reinforcement to prevent erosion; the second year, when an alga bloom discourages swimming; or several years down the road, when the pond needs cleaning out because of silt accumulation. Disregard maintenance at your peril: Unattended ponds like to disappear in a eutrophic soup or run away some dark and stormy night.

Maintenance boils down to keeping an eye on three basics: the watershed, the water itself, and structure. Ideally your watershed will deliver water with a minimum of sediment, alga- and weed-feeding nutrients, and contaminants. The pond itself will have been designed to minimize aquatic weeds and algae, particularly by eliminating excessively shallow areas. Inflows and outflows will discourage erosion. Piping systems, if any, will not leak. Pervious soil in the structure will be minimal, either by nature or after lining with a sealant (clay or bentonite usually) or a membrane. Water exchange will be sufficient to prevent stagnation and excessively high summer temperatures. And fish and other aquatic crops will not be the source of pond degradation. Alas, few ponds meet all these standards.

Checklist for a Healthy Pond

- Inflow volume is adequate.
- Inflow is clean.
- Inflow silt is minimal.
- Shore grade is adequate.
- Basin depth is adequate.
- Water temperature is healthy (will depend on fish crop and stratification).
- Outflow is reinforced.
- Embankment (if any) is sturdy.
- Piping (if any) functions well; no leaks.
- Fish and other live inhabitants are healthy, not causing problems.
- Vegetation (submerged and emergent) is in balance.

Water Quality

The problem most common to pond owners is an excess of algae and/or aquatic weeds. Some kind of alga or vegetative growth is inevitable in most ponds; in fact it's desirable. Without it the pond wouldn't support frogs, salamanders, fish, and other

Alga happens. It's the result of rich aquatic fertility (mostly phosphorous and organic matter), and if you're interested only in attracting wild animals and waterfowl, it may be of little concern. Some critters find it delicious. But if your pond is used for recreation or raising fish, too much algae makes swimming a nightmare, and as it decays it uses up the oxygen necessary for healthy fish. Algae control is usually accomplished by dredging, aeration, infusions of fresh water, biological control (such as grass carp or crawfish), or a combination thereof.

forms of attractive pond life. But when macrophytes (better known as weeds) or algae begin to interfere with swimming and fishing, it's time to draw the line.

Nutrients, particularly phosphorous and nitrogen, feed aquatic vegetation. This "fertilizer" may be entering the pond from the watershed or it may already be present in the pond soil. Probably it's a little of both. A pond sited downstream from fertilized fields is a common example of a pond primed for alga and weed problems. Other sources of unwanted watershed nutrients include septic system runoff and storm water or road drainage. A good look at your watershed and inflow/outflow streams will help you detect unwanted nutrients. Beware green slime growing in the waterways. If watershed runoff is determined to be a source of excess nutrients, take steps to eliminate the problem. Perhaps you can divert the water away from the pond, or remove the source of watershed nutrients.

When this isn't possible, or of significant effect, water treatment or biological control may be necessary. Biological controls include live bacteria as well as using foraging critters such as crawfish and carp. Chemical algicides, while effective, treat only the symptoms and thus should be considered a last resort. Dyes can be used to cut off sunlight from nuisance plants. The downside is that the dye eliminates all vegetative growth, wiping out the food source for most pond life, and dousing the pond and downstream watershed with chemicals to boot.

In-pond phosphorous and other organic matter are the principal sources of nutrients. They're usually present in the pond soil, particularly sediment that may have accumulated over the years from runoff, vegetative decay and fish waste, and atmospheric pollution. The first question I ask clients with an alga-macrophyte problem is, What's the pond history? How long ago was it built? What kind of fish or other crops might have been grown here? What's been coming down the watershed? It's not unusual for a 10-year-old pond to accumulate enough organic matter to trigger a weed problem. In fact, eutrophication—the natural death process of a pond—begins the first day.

In addition to nourishing algae, incoming sediment displaces water, especially around the inflow area. A silt catchment pool dug in the waterway just upstream from the pond will trap a lot of this sediment before it reaches the pond, and can be cleaned out periodically. Filter fabrics can be hung across inflow channels to intercept silt.

An unhealthy increase in sediment fertility (organic matter in the pondbed soil) can occur because of pond stratification. Stratification occurs when the water forms distinct layers of varying temperature, warm above, cold below. The colder layer is low in oxygen, which inhibits the natural decomposition of organic matter, resulting in a long-term accumulation of phosphorous and other nutrients. Come summer, warmer temperatures and wind-mixed water make oxygen available below, releasing nutrients and triggering vegetative growth.

Dredging out sediment is an effective way to reduce nutrients. Working in the dry bed after the pond has been drained or pumped is preferable to dredging a full pond. A less expensive alternative is to use aeration to mix thermal layers—adding oxygen to the bottom to help decompose organic matter. In ponds used for fish culture, aeration not only provides continuing nutrient control, but enhances fish growth with supplementary oxygen as well. Water "conditioners" also will remove phosphorous from the water and stimulate bacterial activity, thus hastening decomposition of nutrients. For example, aluminum sulfate used as a water conditioner reduces alga growth: Binding with phosphorous, it acts like a precipitate, causing the phosphorous and algae to drop and the water to clear. Aluminum sulfate will only work within a certain pH, and the water should be tested first. Use extreme caution: Aluminum compounds can have toxic effects on pond fish and biota.

If fish are not a necessity, it may be better to do without them. Uneaten fish food and fish wastes quickly become alga fertilizer. Equally damaging, fish feed on zooplankton, which would otherwise eat up algae. However, some fish can help eliminate unwanted vegetation. Grass carp are voracious vegetarians, and are stocked in many states to keep ponds and lakes weed-free. (Some states prohibit carp; check with your Fish and Wildlife Department.) Crawfish also eat up macrophytes (see Clean Up with Crawfish, page 58–60.)

Weeds and algae need light in order to grow, hence the connection between vegetation and clear, shallow water. Not only do nuisance plants like shallow, well-lit water, but they also like the warmer temperatures

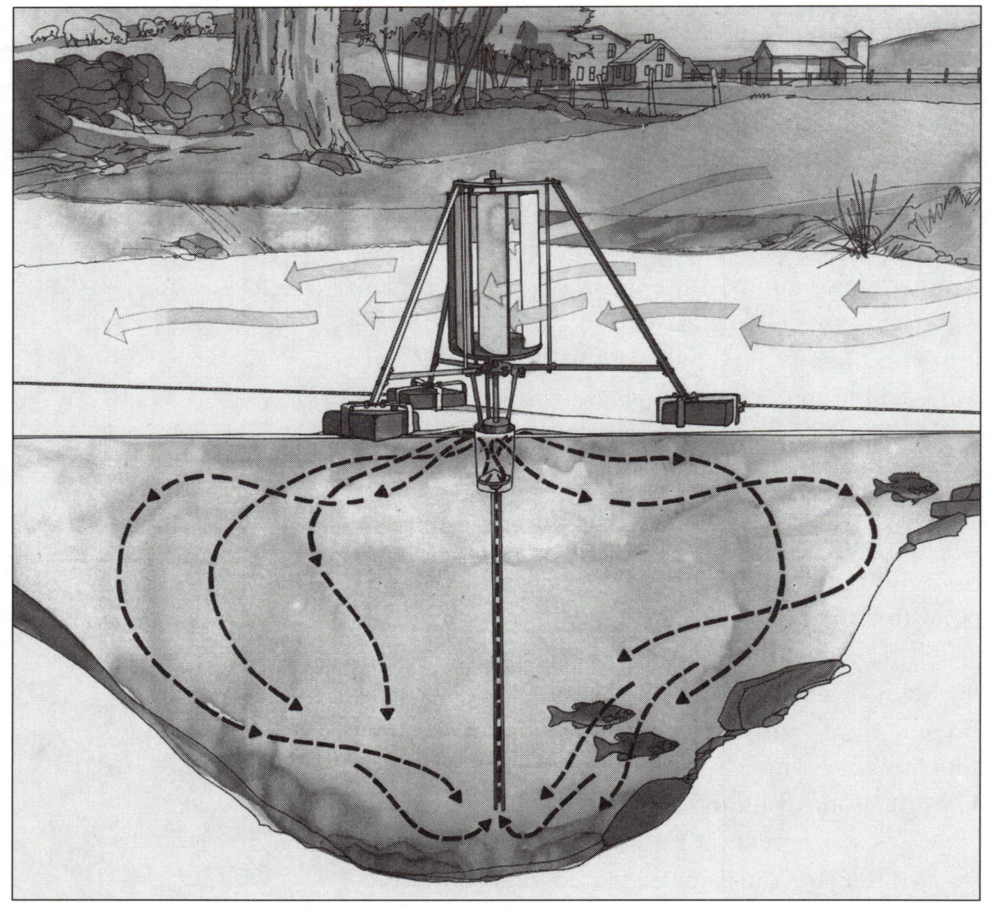

FRANK FRETZ

This wind-powered aerator pulls bottom water to the surface, aerates it, and releases it—increasing oxygen levels and preventing temperature stratification. However, if you're raising a lot of fish, keep in mind that the worst heat and oxygen conditions often occur when there's no wind.

there. Eliminating shallow water goes a long way to reducing alga and weed problems.

You can also control algae and weeds through the temporary reduction of water levels. Drawdowns of several feet expose aquatic roots to the unfriendly effects of sun and air and frost. They also allow the pond owner to rake up desiccated vegetation, eliminating further sources of nutrients. Unfortunately, the beneficial effects of a drawdown may be relatively short-lived; often restored water levels restore the weeds.

Adding clean supplementary water to the pond also discourages vegetative growth. Additional water usually helps oxygenate and cool the pond. Whenever possible, add supplementary water with a waterfall effect, further oxygenating the pond and stirring the water.

Another technique involves drawing the overflow from the bottom layer of water rather than from the top. Overflow from the lower layer is lower in oxygen and richer in nutrients, which alga-troubled ponds can do without. To draw the overflow from the bottom, use a siphon or a more elaborate permanent spillway system designed for this purpose. If no overflow exists, a pump can be used to pull up deep water and splash it back in, creating a healthful oxygenating effect as well as mixing the temperature layers.

Many pond owners are having success using live bacteria to accelerate decomposition of organic matter. The idea is to establish a biological base to compete with algae and break down sediment and sludge.

Given the multitude of potential solutions to water-quality problems, the inevitable question is, Where do I begin? That depends on the function of the pond and the stubbornness of the trouble. A pond used only occasionally will get different treatment from one more frequently used, one in which fish are dying, or one being used to raise a commercial crop. I tend to begin with the least expensive, least intrusive, nonchemical treatments. Can you fix the pond simply by digging out the edges? By adding an easy-to-deliver water supply? By digging a simple catchment pool? By throwing in some crawfish to eat the algae? Often, the answer is yes. Save the more intrusive remedies for life or death emergencies.

Structure

Water-quality problems can produce unattractive views and lousy swimming, but that's small potatoes compared to the negative potential of structural defects. Embankment ponds in particular are vulnerable to construction flaws, leaks, erosion, and pest damage, which unchecked can lead to severe damage or even total failure. The term *dammed pond* takes on a whole new connotation when you think about embankment failures.

The lesson of pond blowouts is pretty basic. It's one thing to excavate a dug-out pond and let it fill with water; building an embankment pond by lifting water above the existing terrain with a dam is a different kettle of fish. Dams should be built by qualified

The remains of an improperly constructed pond spillway system. Here, a horizontal culvert was installed in loose soil, without antiseep collars, and washed out during spring runoff. This is not only damaging to the pond but potentially dangerous to downstream inhabitants as well.

Erosion Solutions

Pond feeder streams often require reinforcement to prevent erosion, especially in large watersheds. Two different approaches to using reinforcing stone are shown here. On the left, crushed rock (riprap) has been used; on the right, fieldstone. Crushed rock usually can be ordered from a local supplier and delivered to the spot. It's often used in an emergency, after a bad bout of erosion. Fieldstone has a more natural appearance and can be gathered during pond construction.

FRANK FRETZ

An earth-cut spillway, reinforced with stone to minimize erosion, is best located at the side of an earthen dam where the dam's newly packed earth joins an undisturbed ground surface.

contractors, keeping in mind that in this case, small is not beautiful. A good, thick embankment base on a solid foundation beats a skinny dam any day. Core trenches, good spillways, and well-drained, track-packed material are your insurance against dam failure. So is careful matching of the structure with the watershed, as well as periodic inspections. Watch out for erosion: Make sure the overflow is not eroding the embankment and that root damage from nearby trees isn't compromising the structure. If you're not comfortable acting as your own dam inspector, have a local contractor do it periodically.

Embankment erosion is most likely to occur around the outlet or spillway, which is usually a piped or earthen overflow system. Primary spillways that run over the surface of the dam or pond rim must be carefully installed and protected against erosion with fieldstone, crushed rock, or other reinforcing materials. Outlets piped through the embankment should be watched to make sure water isn't leaking around the exterior of the pipe, leading to erosion, leakage, and perhaps dam failure. Concrete dams should be monitored for signs of deterioration in the dam and leaks around the footings or seams. Concrete dams have a habit of leaking through the base. Outlets—both piped and open channel—can be quickly plugged by beavers, threatening the integrity of the dam. Embankments may also suffer damage from burrowing muskrats, and even crawfish, in which case you'll have to eradicate these critters from your pond.

This Is Not a Swimming Pool

In my work I see a lot of ponds, and, perhaps more significantly, a lot of pond owners. Many of them have real problems, insufficient water and invasive vegetation topping the list. But a surprising amount are unhappy with perfectly adequate ponds. A small clump of cattails, water levels that temporarily drop a foot at the height of summer, cloudy water: These minor blemishes drive some people nuts. They're ready to rebuild the pond or douse it with chemicals to achieve The Perfect Look. Of course, there's no such thing. I do my best to convince them that we're not talking about a swimming pool here, and equally important, if it ain't broke, don't fix it. And please, whatever you do, don't dredge out the inside face of the dam to eliminate a few weeds without considering what effect it might have on water retention.

If, however, you've got a hunch that your pond is going to blow (the spillway is crumbling and there's a 50-year-frequency rainfall forecast, for instance), deal with it. Fast. Get the water out of the pond. If the pond has a drain, use it. If not, get someone with a pump to unload the water and then hire an excavator to open up the embankment. Your fish won't like it, but your downstream neighbors will.

While we're on the subject of drains, I should emphasize here how useful they are during pond maintenance. Of course, a drain has to have a place to go, so you won't often find drains in excavated ponds. Emptying an excavated pond usually involves pumping, combined, if possible, with cutting off incoming water. Many embankment ponds don't include drains either, but drainage is not limited to pumping. Many an embankment pond can be drained using a siphon, which may involve one or more garden hoses or larger flexible piping. Using a large-diameter flexible pipe with a strong siphon action, it's possible to use the siphon even to suck mud and sediment out of a pond.

Symptoms of a Dying Pond

I'm often asked about the signs of a dying pond. My answer begins with the same question I ask people who plan to design a new pond: What is the pond to be used for? If it's a pond for swimming or for raising trout—the most popular uses for ponds in the North—you'll want clear water and a minimum of weeds and algae. But if you're raising carp or catfish in Missouri, a murky, warm-water pond rich in plankton is the ticket to success.

It's not hard to tell when a pond is in trouble. One of the first signs is a fishkill. Not just a few fish, mind you. Five percent mortality annually is accepted for trout, for instance. But if on a hot, overcast day you find a slew of fish belly-up, it may be that the amount of oxygen in the water has sunk below the level needed to sustain them. An excess of aquatic vegetation dying and burning up oxygen in the process may be the cause. In this case the pond should be drained and cleaned out. Overheated water may also trigger a fishkill. Brook trout begin to die at temperatures above 75 degrees F. A new source of water may be required. Sometimes immediate aeration of the water will stop a fishkill. An outboard motor or a pump recirculating the water can do the trick in a hurry. A better solution may involve a permanent aeration system, a deeper basin to increase the volume of water, or a hardier species of fish. Pollution also causes fishkills. If toxic runoff from the watershed around the pond is a problem, it can be deflected with diversionary ditches.

Acid precipitation, especially in the Northeast, has been responsible for killing many ponds and lakes. Ironically, acidified ponds appear "healthy" because they are crystal clear, a quality we appreciate in our drinking water and therefore assume is good in other waters. But a pond that is crystal clear is only that way because nothing will grow there. To determine whether acidity is a problem, it may be necessary to have the pH of the water checked by a laboratory. Fish grow best at a pH between 6.5 and 9.0. Acidic water may be corrected by adding 20-mesh limestone. Consult your State Extension Service for suggested dosages. An application permit may be required.

The empty pond blues can usually be traced back to one common oversight—no test pits. The soil in this embankment was simply too sandy to hold water above groundwater level. A remedy may be found by adding a clay liner, membrane, or soil sealer; or perhaps by introducing supplementary water. Good luck.

Clean water is not necessarily clear water. Aquatic vegetation generates oxygen and provides cover and food for pond life. Excessive alga and weed growth can destroy the beauty and usefulness of a pond, however. If left unchecked, an infestation can lead to stagnation, higher water temperatures, off-taste and disease in fish, and fishkills.

Remedies for alga and weed infestation include physical removal (skimmers, rakes, digging, and pulling), biological controls (bacterial solutions and weed-eating fish like the silver carp), drawdowns, and dredging. Aeration and supplementary sources of fresh water can also help reduce aquatic vegetation. Chemical algicides are available but are likely to cause more of a problem than the one they cure.

Leaks are another prime cause of pond-owner distress. What causes them? How do you fix them? They're not as easy to spot as dead fish and algae. A pond mysteriously fails to fill up, or the water level drops unexpectedly. Is it a leak? The question should be, Is it a *bad* leak? In a natural pond, water seeps out of the basin as naturally as water drips through a coffee filter. As long as the inflow exceeds the outflow (from seepage and evaporation), you have little to worry about. But if a pond is not holding enough water, one of two problem areas may be at the root of the trouble: defects in the pond basin material or flaws in construction. If the problem lies in the basin itself, it is likely that the soil is too porous, allowing water to seep out through the entire structure. You can determine whether the soil lining your pond is too porous by analyzing its clay content, which should be somewhere between 10 and 20 percent (see Simple Soil Test, page 22).

If the soil appears to have a high enough clay content, your problem may be a more localized leak caused by a streak of sand, a deposit of shale or gravel, or perhaps a fissure in an underlying ledge. Sometimes it is possible to spot a point where water is seeping through to the outside of the pond embankment. Vegetation is often richer around a leak. Occasionally dyes are used to trace leaks, and dowsers have also proved helpful in detecting hidden outflows. I know a contractor who uses scuba gear to dive underwater and look for suspicious "holes," and then drops flour over the spot to see whether it drifts toward the leak. The Dutch use airborne infrared imaging to check for potential problems in dikes.

Symptoms of a Dying Pond

- Fishkill
- Siltation
- Excessive algae and/or vegetation
- Leaks
- Loss of water source
- Erosion

If the leak isn't serious, you may be able to fix it yourself. In a small pond it's possible to cover pervious areas with patches of PVC, or to drain the pond and add a sealant. For the most part, however, a serious leak will require some help from a contractor.

Whether a leak is general or localized, the standard remedy is to drain the pond dry and seal it with clay. Clay is customarily trucked to the pond site, spread, and packed down by a bulldozer or a sheepsfoot roller. If good clay is available locally, it's probably your best and most economical solution. Clay is usually added in applications of a foot in thickness—sometimes more—which effectively rules it out for small ponds, which would be significantly reduced in size. For those who live in areas where good clay is not readily available, bentonite is an alternative. Bentonite is a natural clay sealant that swells dramatically when wet. You can purchase it in powder or granular form, often through a local well-driller or a well-drilling-supply firm. Bentonite is applied "in the dry" at a rate of 1 pound per square foot, mixed with the pond basin material with a light harrow, then packed down. Simply dumping it from a rowboat into a leaky pond is unlikely to remedy the problem. Bentonite can also be purchased embedded in fabric rolls. Unfortunately, if the pond is fed by subsurface springs, clay or bentonite liners may plug up the water source. Polymer emulsions also can be used to seal ponds (see Resources, pages 62–63).

Liners made of sheet plastic—usually PVC—constitute the ultimate artificial water barrier. Their chief drawback, besides their expense (45 to 50 cents per square foot for a 20-mil sheet), is that they are easily punctured. Also, on occasion, they billow up to the pond's surface when groundwater seeps underneath them. Because of these and other potential complications, liners are usually reserved for small garden ponds. However, you may decide to install drains underneath the membrane to eliminate hydrostatic pressure from below.

No matter how well it's made, a pond without a sufficient source of water will never fill up. Getting more water to the pond may involve bringing in supplemental water by pipe or ditch from a nearby stream or spring, preferably so the water flows to the pond with the aid of gravity. If there is sufficient runoff above the pond, it may be worthwhile to dig diversion ditches to feed the pond. Feeder ditches should be reinforced to protect the land from erosion and to protect the pond from siltation.

Finally, leakage may occur through faulty spillway piping. Older ponds are particularly vulnerable to leakage where drains or standpipes have deteriorated. Even in cases where the pipes themselves are not leaking, water can find its way out around the exterior of a pipe—especially where antiseep collars were not installed. If the pipe is leaking, it should be removed, replaced, or repaired, usually by a professional contractor. While you're at it, make sure the pipe is collared with antiseep baffles. In the case of a defective trickle tube, some pond owners forgo the repair expenses and instead pour concrete down the tube to permanently plug it; this should be done only if a satisfactory overflow can be substituted. Sometimes, surface overflows are substituted for defective pipe systems; they're less expensive, less likely to leak, and offer the bonus of providing a visible stream area, often a good site for landscaping. A surface overflow attractively lined with fieldstone can be shaped into a waterfall and flanked with attractive water-loving plants, such as ferns and daylilies.

New Life for Old Ponds

A good example of aquatic rejuvenation is a ¼-acre embankment pond that I worked on not long ago. The pond lies in a clearing near the bottom of a wooded hillside. It had been commissioned by my neighbor Bill 10 years ago, and was built by a local contractor.

Bill wanted me to look over the pond. He was having trouble and had started to drain it. It was late summer, before the fall rains: a good time for pond repairs. I thought we could accomplish something before wet weather muddied up the basin too much for excavation work.

Bill had plans to build a house overlooking the pond—but not in its present condition. The water level was down a foot, and the water was thickly clouded and flecked across the surface with mushy green algae. Bill told me the history of the structure. After construction, the pond had performed well. The water was clear and cold, about 10 feet deep in the center—good for swimming. Bill had stocked trout, but the fish mysteriously died. I asked him how soon after excavation the trout had been stocked. He couldn't recall. What variety of trout were they? Again he didn't remember. I told him that it would be tough to diagnose the trouble without those details. Pond keeping is like gardening: You need records in order to keep track of crops and structural details, and to correct errors and make improvements.

I did offer some conjecture. Perhaps the fish had been stocked too soon. It's important to delay stocking a new pond until at least a year after construction, because the initial decomposition of organic matter in the basin eats up oxygen and produces gases lethal to fish. And depending on the temperature of the water, one variety of trout may survive while another dies.

Bill continued his story. After the trout died, he had a visitor: "This joker tells me, 'Hey, watch this,' and he throws in a couple of goldfish he'd bought at Woolworth's. Well, the summer after that there were a few more goldfish, and the summer after that the pond was

FRANK FRETZ

Groundwater seeping through the ledge at left will fill a dugout pond. But where the water table is low, exposed ledge can drain a pond.

packed with them! You couldn't even swim without them bumping into you. It was awful."

Goldfish are fast breeders and voracious bottom feeders, like their cousins, the carp, and they had stirred the pond into a turbid slurry. With some help from his wife and two daughters, Bill drained the pond and killed the fish. It was not a pleasant task. At first the drain wouldn't open, so Bill strapped on an Aqua-Lung and dived down to investigate. He saw that the gate valve had jammed under a pile of silt. He did not attempt to open the valve manually because of the danger of being held underwater by the suction—a wise decision on his part, considering the number of accidental deaths that result from the strong pull of a suddenly opened underwater drainpipe. Bill later managed to open the valve from the outside by ramming a steel pipe into the drain and popping the valve open. As the pond emptied, the goldfish collected in a shallow pool, from which they were dispatched one by one.

Then Bill noticed that the pile of silt covering the drain had come in from the stream that fed the pond. A delta of silt had spread out to the middle of the basin. "I used to be able to dive from that rock," he said, pointing to a boulder on the shore. "It's too shallow now." I told him that the silt had been contributing to the turbidity of the water as much as the bottom-feeding goldfish had. Not to mention spoiling his diving.

Bill and I also trekked through his pond's watershed upstream. A swampy tract of land, it looked like a delicious source of nutrients for the algae and plankton that choked the water. It was also the source of the silt that was filling the pond.

As it turned out, cleaning up Bill's pond was a straightforward matter. First it had to be drained once again. A backhoe-bulldozer team was hired for two days to scrape up the silt and truck it to a spot near Bill's garden, for use as a top dressing and landscape fill. There was enough time for the backhoe operator to dig a desilting pool in the path of the stream feeding the pond, about 10 yards from shore. Omitting the desilting pool during the original construction had been a major oversight. Now the silt that had been filling the pond and roiling the water would settle in the pool, which could be cleaned out without disturbing the pond itself. A layer of crushed stone was spread in the stream near the pond to further inhibit erosion. The pond was then allowed to fill. I suggested to Bill that in a year he stock the pond with rainbow trout. That species is the most tolerant of temperature fluctuations and the most stress resistant of the trout family, and might help gobble up organic matter that would otherwise nurture algae. But no more goldfish.

Do Your Homework

Erosion-proofing the feeder stream is a common remedy for sick ponds. In another case I worked on recently, Clifton's small embankment pond was in desperate need of work along the inflow, which had been dug to catch runoff in order to fill the pond. The ditch was deeply eroded, and I suggested that Clifton bring in a couple of truckloads of stone to reinforce the banks. Perhaps a concrete sluiceway would be needed to stanch the flow of eroding soil. A small silt-catching pool would be helpful, too.

Clifton's troubles extended beyond the feeder stream, however. There was a small leak in the dam, and the horizontal water-level spillway pipe had clogged, sending overflow cascading across the embankment. That overflow was causing severe structural erosion. Besides that, Clifton was concerned about several dying birch trees along the top of the dam. "Almost as soon as we started digging, some of them died," he told me. "I had to cut one down, and it really made me cry. I feel like I'm messing up the environment."

Clifton had made a mistake common among pond builders. In order to minimize damage to the landscape, he'd neglected to clear the site properly. Those trees should have been cut before he had the pond dug. It's a cliché, but you've got to break eggs to make an omelet. Now the trees were going to die anyway. Their roots had been damaged during the excavation, and they'd been flooded by the water in the pond. The roots would soon rot and lead to further leakage in the dam.

Clifton had intended to build a pond surrounded by trees. Unfortunately, nobody had advised him that the trees were too close. His pond had been excavated with the barest clearing around the site, and consequently the dam turned out undersized. He could reinforce the dam from the outside with trucked-in fill, although it would be difficult now that the pond structure blocked access to the hill. On the other hand, he could drain the pond and install a membrane liner of plastic or rubber. (He'd tried using clay to remedy the leak, but that hadn't been completely effective.) I left Clifton with a list of potential patchwork solutions, none of which would have been necessary had he cleared the site properly to begin with and put up a sturdy dam.

Choose Your Equipment

Duane's pond was ancient and shallow. We couldn't be sure that it wasn't simply a swamp. Duane assured me, however, that some of the local old-timers remembered it as a fine pond for skating and swimming. It remained a fine skating pond, but you couldn't get me in that water on a bet. It looked like hot chocolate without the marshmallow. The pond lay at the north end of Duane's hayfield, backed up against the edge of the woods. His kids liked to swim in it, but Duane kept scraping his knees. He wanted it deeper. Simple enough, I told him: Drain it and excavate. You'll find out if it was ever really much of a pond. How's that? he asked. If you hit ledge, you'll know it couldn't have been very deep, I said.

A ridge of earth at the downstream end of the pond served as a dam. Duane wondered whether he should tear it open to drain the pond, or pump out the water. I told him that if he breeched the dam, he'd be able to drain the pond thoroughly, and if the digging went well, it would be worth the trouble. He'd be able to excavate more effectively and get the most possible reservoir volume. The more water you have, the more you can do with it. On the other hand, if he hit ledge, it might be impossible to enlarge the pond. The excavated channel through the dam would have been unnecessary. It was a gamble.

The equipment Duane planned to use to dredge the pond figured in the bet, too. If a dragline were used, the dredging could be done without breeching the dam. But draglines are expensive and slow. A bulldozer is usually the most economical way to go; it's fast and relatively cheap. But there hasn't been a bulldozer invented yet that runs underwater.

In the end, Duane compromised. He hired a dragline operator to dredge the pond, which had been partially drained by siphon hose. Not a bit of ledge was encountered. He hadn't breeched the dam, so considerable expense was saved and the integrity of the embankment was guaranteed. The work was accomplished in three days, and Duane wound up with a pond covering ⅓ acre and 8 to 9 feet deep throughout most of the basin.

Water to Go

Silt deposits, leaks, and weeds are the most common problems that plague ponds. Usually those impairments can be remedied. A fourth disorder, however, is difficult to overcome: insufficient water. Most of us have seen examples. A pond with not enough water looks like a backyard gravel pit. Invariably it is the result of improper siting. The builder failed to excavate test holes to determine soil quality and the flow of water through the site.

I was once asked to look over a small sauna pond. The landowner had chosen the pond site because of

Cattails can make an attractive border plant, but left unchecked they can also colonize a pond.

its proximity to his sauna house rather than to an adequate supply of water. There it sat, skillfully chiseled out—and bone dry. "What should I do?" the fellow asked. You could dig a well and pump water to the pond, I said, adding that it might prove to be an expensive solution. I told him that repairing a pond is like remodeling an old house: You have to ask yourself at what point and after how much expense would it be best to tear it down and start from scratch—in the right place. That was the best I could offer. I later heard that he came up with an offbeat solution. For a small fee, the local fire department trucks in water to fill the pond.

Weed the Pond

Weed incursion represents a normal stage in the life of a pond as it evolves into a marsh. Over the years, as shore areas fill in with silt and organic matter, the water becomes shallow and warm, a perfect environment for aquatic plants. Weeds growing in the middle of a pond usually signal that the time for action is at hand, unless you wish to encourage aquatic plants as wildlife cover and feed (see Wildlife, pages 115–20.)

Diligent hand-weeding and mulching can be effective if the area involved is small. Early spring is the best time to pull weeds, before roots are deeply established. Algae should be scooped out of the water with a net. You may wish to reserve a small area for cattails, for aesthetic reasons, but be wary that they don't spread. Otherwise, cattails should be cut, right before flowering, as far below the water surface as possible. Cut and rake up submerged plants as they float to the surface. Waterside Products Corporation (see Resources, page 61) sells a battery-powered hand tool that cuts submerged plants—not emergent grasses or cattails—as much as 12 feet below the surface of the water. Never leave plant debris in the pond or on the banks to decay and wash back into the water.

UV-resistant landscape fabrics developed for use as underwater mulch may be laid over weedy areas and weighted down with rocks or clean sand. Sand alone will effectively smother weeds. Eventually, though, silt will settle on any barrier, providing a medium for new weed and alga growth.

Drawdowns have been a mainstay of pond maintenance for centuries. Aquatic plants cannot live without water, and when the pond is dried out during hot or cold weather, the weeds die. A drawdown of 2 to 4 feet will usually kill shoreline vegetation without harming fish; a complete drawdown will cleanse the entire pond. In areas where frost penetrates the soil by at least 4 inches during winter, the roots of many exposed aquatic plants die. Drawdowns are most effective when you implement them with a drain or gate that keeps the water level down. Otherwise, short-term drawdowns can be accomplished with pumps or siphons. Alas, drawdowns usually result in temporary solutions to weed problems; eventually, the trouble reappears.

Dredging allows you to remove silt and, if necessary, deepen the pond and make the slopes steeper to eliminate weed-prone shallows. You'll get the best results if you drain the pond before dredging. Once dredging is

Lake Smarts

If you've been tearing out your hair over a pond full of invincible algae and weeds, I know of a book for you. Stuart McComas has put together a how-to manual that's valuable for pond owners and for anyone interested in watershed improvement. *Lake Smarts* offers reservoir-tested reviews of tools and techniques for removing nuisance weeds and algae, including rakes, nets, drags, pulp hooks, bedsprings, bottom barriers, containment booms, liquid dyes, and large industrial machines. The author provides sources and costs of all items, and scores of photographs help you judge which tools will best suit your budget and your back.

Other topics that aquatic scientist McComas covers with equal thoroughness include fish habitat improvement; sediment control; on-site wastewater treatment; turbid water; waterfowl attraction; and predator, pest, and insect control. The author never lets us forget that aquatic health involves creatures besides ourselves, and he strikes a balance between our enjoyment and what's best for the natural habitat.

Coproduced by the Terrene Institute and the US Environmental Protection Agency, *Lake Smarts* is a practical guide to solving lake and pond problems ecologically. Try out some of these gadgets and techniques on your next bloom of algae. This book is a must for pond owners. For ordering information, see the Resources section, page 63.

"The basic landscape rake is one of the more versatile lake rakes. It works especially well for sparse weeds and satisfactorily in denser growth. It can also be used to rake in filamentous algae and for raking up weeds that have drifted to shore. You can even use it to smooth out the beach. Since it is a landscape rake, it's also handy around the yard.

"The landscape rake has two drawbacks. Its short teeth fill quickly with weeds, and it takes time to clean them off, which decreases the rake's efficiency. With a full load of weeds, the rake is fairly heavy (between 25 and 50 pounds) . . .

"Another way to control cattails is by drowning them. Cattails use their shoots to bring oxygen down to the roots, so if their roots and shoots are completely submerged, cattails will die and not regrow the following year. One way to thin the cattail growth by drowning is to cut the cattail vegetation that appears above the ice in winter. Water levels usually rise in spring, and if the water level goes above the cattails for a couple of weeks, they will not regrow . . . Cattails are beneficial, however. If you decide to thin them, cut only the minimum necessary to allow boat access or to clear areas for nearshore recreation . . ."

—Excerpted from *Lake Smarts: The First Lake Maintenance Handbook,* The Terrene Institute.

complete, focus on preventive maintenance. The cooler and cleaner the water, the healthier your pond will be. Check your watershed to be sure you have no fertilizer runoff, septic leachate, or other contaminants. If your pond is fed by a stream, dig a small silt pool in the stream channel above the pond. Silt will collect in the pool, which can be periodically cleaned out. If you stock fish, don't feed more than they clean up. To avoid low water in summer, you may want to add water to the pond. Some pond owners use surplus well water or dig another well for the purpose. Finally, highly oxygenated water helps fish thrive and speeds the breakdown of decaying vegetation. Mechanical aerators, fountains, or waterfalls can be installed to increase the oxygen content of the water.

Animals, too, can help keep your environment in balance. Ducks, geese, Israeli carp, grass carp, and crawfish eat aquatic plants. I've had success with crawfish purchased from a bait shop; they eat the submerged and decaying plants and have kept my pond relatively free of algae (see Resources, page 64–65).

Clean Up with Crawfish

Crawfish eat pond weeds. This isn't big news to connoisseurs of jambalaya and crawfish pie, especially in Louisiana, capital of the $30 million annual US crawfish industry, where farmers routinely raise crawfish in flooded fields to clean up the detritus from rice and other aquatic crops. But it may come as a welcome surprise to those pond owners who think of crawfish as bait and nothing more.

A recent study by aquacultural researchers at the State University of New York (SUNY) at Brockport reported that crawfish, when present in high enough density, are effective at eliminating submerged vegetation (macrophytes), belieing the need for toxic chemicals, elaborate aeration systems, unnatural-looking dyes, dredging, or any of the other "cures" for nuisance pond vegetation. You can achieve the needed density by a high rate of stocking, or—less expensively—by allowing a smaller population to multiply naturally. In theory, the crawfish will thrive until they eliminate the vegetative feed and then drop back to a lower, sustainable rate. However, if predatory fish or birds are present, the crawfish may not reach sufficient numbers to handle the weed problem. Alas, the stocking density required to control filamentous algae in larger lakes troubled by aquatic plants such as Eurasian milfoil and water chestnut would appear to be cost-prohibitive. Crawfish seem best suited to control pond algae.

I can confirm the SUNY study, after adding crawfish to my own alga-plagued pond several years ago. For several summers I had watched the pond become increasingly vulnerable to blooms of algae and weeds at the peak of the season, when high temperatures and low water exchange encourage temporary bursts of vegetation. As the pond aged, it accumulated additional sediment that further nourished unwanted growth.

I have always rejected the use of chemical weed controls because of their potential toxic side effects on plant and animal (including human) life, which left me with few options other than manual removal (dredging, raking, skimming) or drawdowns to starve out the weeds. Aeration, through either water recirculation or oxygen injection, seemed like a complicated and expensive option for me, with no guarantees. Dyes, liquid biological digesters, and pondbed liners to mulch out growth never fit the Keep It Simple operating credo for my pond. I had been tempted by tales of grass- and alga-eating carp, but they turned out to be illegal to import to many states, including my own.

I did try a partial dredging of the basin to eliminate one shallow area conducive to algae. The algae disappeared, but only temporarily. I did other things to discourage aquatic growth, including eliminating feed for the trout I sometimes stock and using a net to skim off the offensive green scum. I bought a pair of geese for their well-known weed-eating skills, and they indeed cleaned up the water, but they turned the pond into their own Porta-potty, clearly a cure worse than the disease. I finally threw in the towel and went down the road to a weed-free lake for my August swims.

I first heard about crawfish from a friend who runs a tackle shop. He was enthusiastic about their culinary potential as well as their use as bait, adding that where he'd seen them growing in Vermont, the ponds were weed-free. I did some research. There are more than 300 species of crawfish in the United States. In the South, the large Louisiana red variety is grown for the table. In the North, several smaller species are cultured for bait. Nobody mentioned using them intentionally to control algae, but there were warnings that burrowing crawfish may cause seepage problems as well as turbid water. Considering the state my pond was in already, I decided to risk it.

I ordered a batch of red swamp crawfish from an out-of-state supplier, but they arrived very nearly parboiled after a cross-country UPS trip. I stocked them anyway, but a better word would be interred. I never saw them again. I later learned that Vermont is probably too far north for red swamp crawfish to overwinter, which the supplier hadn't mentioned. Oddly enough, the same thing happened the next summer with a bucketful of native crawfish I'd purchased from a local bait shop. They disappeared, too. We had another bad bout of algae. I assumed I didn't have the right habitat for successful crawfish culture.

The following spring, I began to notice burrows and tunnel entries near rocks just offshore. The water appeared more turbid than usual. Dismembered claws and molted shells started to appear. My children found tiny crawfish scurrying across the beach. All this, coincidentally, as we began to experience a severe drought combined with a heat wave. Perfect weather for algae. I looked for signs of aquatic growth, but the cloudy water obscured the view. I kept waiting for the weeds and scum to explode. It never happened. The few leeches we had also disappeared, and I have since heard that crawfish are great leech-busters.

In fact, the closer I looked, the less vegetation I found. By the end of the year, the bottom looked as virginal as it had after excavation—raw mud. The kids began catching crawfish of all sizes, from tiny little offspring to 4-inch microlobsters. While neighboring pond owners fought their usual summer battles with algae, we swam unscathed. I bought a minnow trap and enlarged one hole to 3 inches, baited it with a hot dog, and caught a bucketful of crawfish. My kids begged me not to cook them, so I donated them to a friend who had his own problem with algae.

A world full of solutions this simple would be a wonderful one indeed. Alas, there are complications. Nonnative species of crawfish have been introduced to lakes in North America and Europe, where they not only cleaned up the weeds, but they wiped out all other vegetation as well, destroying the food sources for other aquatic critters including fish and waterfowl, and even the smaller native crawfish. Dr. Walter Momot, of Lakehead University, Thunder Bay, Ontario, told me about a couple of provincial lakes lost to nonnative crawfish. He warned me to be careful when stocking crawfish for alga control: "When these [nonnative] babies get in, they clean house. You've got wall-to-wall crawfish." Spanish rice farmers have lost their growing ponds to exotic species of crawfish, as have wild-rice growers in the upper Midwest. Dr. Joseph Makarewicz, one of the authors of the crawfish cropping study at SUNY, told me that the New York State Environmental Resources board cut off its experiments out of fear that nonnative species might escape the control cages and colonize state lakes. I hear the same concerns voiced by state natural resources staff across the country, and I wouldn't be surprised to find increasing prohibitions against importing "exotic" crawfish across state lines. While some crawfish growers caution that in small ponds bass and sunnies eliminate crawfish, hinting at a natural cleanup mechanism, the message appears to be: Use native crawfish to control algae.

Right now, crawfish are the dominant species in my pond. Kingfisher and heron have thinned the population some, and I plan to reintroduce trout, to further control their density. The object is to create a biological equilibrium of fish and crustaceans, minus the weeds and algae. And one day, when the kids are in school, I'm going to trap some crawfish and find out what makes these Louisiana corn and crawfish boils so famous.

Resources

EQUIPMENT & TECHNICAL SUPPORT

The following aquacultural suppliers offer a variety of products including aeration equipment, pumps, water conditioners, and piping.

Aquacenter, Inc.
166 Seven Oaks Road
Leland, MS 38756
1-800-748-8921

Aquatic Eco-Systems, Inc.
1767 Benbow Court
Apopka, FL 32703
1-800-422-3939

Eagar, Inc.
PO Box 540476
North Salt Lake, UT 84054
1-800-423-6249

Stoney Creek Equipment Co.
11073 Peach Avenue
Grant, MI 49327
1-800-448-3873

Waterside Products Corporation
PO Box 876
Lake Mahopac, NY 10541
1-800-552-1217

Aeration Equipment

Air-O-Lator
8100 Paseo
Kansas City, MO 64131
1-800-821-3177

Grovehac, Inc.
4310 North 126th Street
Brookfield, WI 53005
414-781-5020

Hedlund Aquaculture
PO Box 305
Medford, WI 54451
1-800-993-4213

Otterbine Barebo, Inc.
3840 Main Road East
Emmaus, PA 18049
1-800-237-8837

Power House
20 Gwynns Mill Court
Owing Mills, MD 21117
410-654-9700

The following companies specialize in windpowered aerators, water pumps, circulators, and deicers.

Lake Aid Systems
Box 1262
Bismarck, ND 58501
701-738-1355

Malibu Water Resources
P.O. Box 5155
Beverly Hills, CA 90210
1-800-470-4602
www.malibuwater.com
Wind and solar trout pond aeration

O'Brock Windmills
North Benton, OH 44449
330-584-4681

Pondmaster
PO Box 810
Sibley Industries, Inc.
Anderson, MO 64831
1-800-467-6065

Erosion Control Fabrics

BioFence
15 Mohawk Avenue East
Freetown, MA 02717
508-763-5253

Bon Terra
355 West Chestnut Street
Genesee, ID 83832
1-800-882-9489

Indian Valley Industries, Inc.
PO Box 810
Johnson City, NY 13790
1-800-659-5111

T.C. Mirafi
3500 Parkway Lane, Suite 500
Norcross, GA 30092
1-800-234-0484

Synthetic Industries
4019 Industry Drive
Chattanooga, TN 37416
1-800-621-0444

Pond Piping and Outlet Systems

Agri-Drain Corporation
PO Box 458
1462 340th Street
Adair, IA 50002
1-800-232-4742

Pond Dam Piping, Ltd.
398 Eighth Street
Macon, GA 31201
1-800-333-2611

Water Analysis Equipment

Hach Company
PO Box 389
Loveland, CO 80539
1-800-227-4224

LaMotte
PO Box 329
Chestertown, MD 21620
410-778-3100

Water Conditioners

ABA
Water Quality Science International, Inc.
PO Box 552
Bolivar, MO 65613
1-800-558-9442

Aquashade
Cygnet Enterprises, Inc.
1860 Bagwell St.
Flint, MI 48503
1-800-359-7531
www.cygnetenterprises.com

Bacta-Pur/DePhos
Aquatic Eco-Systems, Inc.
1767 Benbow Court
Apopka, FL 32703
1-800-422-3939

Lake Colorant WSP
Becker-Underwood, Inc.
801 Dayton Avenue
Ames, IA 50010
1-800-232-5907

Natural Solutions
P.O. Box 114
Keuka Park, NY 14478-0114
315-531-8803

Source of barley straw bundles for natural algae control

Rapid Klear & Super Bugs
Enviro-Reps International
2646 Palma Drive #445
Ventura, CA 93003
805-650-3563

Sealants and Artificial Membranes

DLM Plastics
1530 Harvard Avenue
Findlay, OH 45840
1-800-444-5877

Resource Conservation
Technology, Inc.
2633 North Calvert Street
Baltimore, MD 21218
410-366-1146

Poly-Flex
2000 West Marshall Drive
Grand Prairie, TX 75051
1-800-527-3322

Reef Industries, Inc.
PO Box 750245
Houston, TX 77275-0245
1-800-231-2417

Yunker Plastics
PO Box 190
Lake Geneva, WI 53147
1-800-236-3328

The following companies specialize in sealants for pervious soils.

CIM Industries
94 Grove Street
Peterborough, NH 03458
1-800-543-3458

Liquid-applied rubber.

Seepage Control, Inc.
PO Box 51177
Phoenix, AZ 85076-1177
1-800-214-9640

Liquid-applied polymer emulsion.

CETCO
521 East Epsom Road, Unit 1-B
Towson, MD 21286
410-339-7424

Bentonite products.

BOOKS & OTHER PUBLICATIONS

Farm Pond Harvest Magazine
1390 North 14500 E Road
Momence, IL 60954
815-472-2686

Abundant information for pond owners, with back issues available; worth a subscription.

A Guide to Management of Small Lakes and Ponds in Illinois
Illinois Department of Conservation
Division of Fisheries
Springfield, IL 62706
502-564-4336

How to Identify Water Weeds and Algae: A Guide to Water Management
Cygnet Enterprises, Inc.
1860 Bagwell St.
Flint, MI 48503
1-800-359-7531
www.cygnetenterprises.com

Lake Smarts: The First Lake Maintenance Handbook
The Terrene Institute
4 Herbert Street
Alexandria VA 22305
703-548-5473

$18.95 plus $4 shipping and handling.

Land and Water Magazine
PO Box 1197
Fort Dodge, IA 50510
515-576-3191

Management of Lakes and Ponds
by George W. Bennett
Krieger Publishing Co.
PO Box 9542
Melbourne, FL 32902
407-724-9542

Comprehensive text on aquatic habitats, fish management, and water quality control. Recommended.

Pond Boss Magazine
P.O. Box 12
Sadler, TX 76264
903-564-6144
www.pondboss@texoma.net

Restoration and Management of Lakes and Reservoirs
by Cooke, Welch, Peterson, and Newroth
Lewis Publishers / CRC Press, Inc.
2000 Corporate Blvd., NW
Boca Raton, FL 33431
407-998-9114

Solid academic reference.

Runoff Report Newsletter
National Nonpoint Source Federation
PO Box 25
1400 16th Street, NW
Washington, DC 20036
202-797-7720

A good source of information about watershed protection.

MISCELLANEOUS

Forestry Suppliers, Inc.
PO Box 8397
Jackson, MS 39284-8397
1-800-647-5368

Offers an impressive catalog of outdoor equipment, including many items of use to pond owners—water-testing equipment, soil-sampling equipment, and landscaping tools, for example.

Izaak Walton League of America
707 Conservation Lane
Gaithersburg, MD 20878-2983
301-548-0150

Nonprofit conservation organization, including "Save Our Streams" program to help monitor, restore, and protect watersheds.

Crawfish

SUPPLIES & INFORMATION

The following companies offer crawfish traps and seines, which can be used to catch crawfish.

Horton's Aquatic Supply
PO Box 432
Lonoke, AR 72086
1-800-503-9985

Memphis Net and Twine Co., Inc.
2481 Matthews Avenue
PO Box 8331
Memphis, TN 38108
1-800-238-6380

A good local bait shop should be able to supply crawfish, or at least steer you in the right direction—probably to the nearest river, under a rock. Otherwise, try these suppliers.

Aquatic Hatcheries
24259 Walnut Point Road
Chestertown, MD 21620
410-778-3518

Northeastern Biologists, Inc.
1 Kerr Road
Rhinebeck, NY 12572
914-876-3983

Real Outdoors Company
10422 North Road
Tomahawk, WI 54487
715-453-4225

Zetts Fish Farm and Hatcheries
Route 53
Drifting, PA 16834
814-345-5357

BOOKS & OTHER PUBLICATIONS

Control and Management of Burrowing Crayfish in Virginia Ponds
by Helfrich, Bryant, and Garling
Ext. Pub. #MT10H
Department of Fisheries and Wildlife Sciences
Virginia Polytechnic Institute and State University
Blacksburg, VA 24061
540-231-5573

Multiple Use Impoundments for Attracting Waterfowl and Producing Crawfish
by Nassar, Zwank, Hayden, Huner
US Department of the Interior Fish and Wildlife Service
National Wetlands Research Center
700 Cajundome Boulevard
Lafayette, LA 70506
318-266-8500

Available from Crawfish Research Center; see next.

Crawfish Research Center
PO Box 44650
University of Southwestern Louisiana
Lafayette, LA 70504
318-482-5239

3. ACTIVITIES AND USE

Our kids were not taking to water like ducks, or anything else, in spite of the front-yard pond and our flotilla of rubber rafts and old inner tubes. Gently my wife would swish them around in the water, but as soon as she plunked them down in the shallows they scrambled out of the water, back up the grassy embankment. This went on for a couple of summers, until the day we visited the public beach. Suddenly the girls were amphibians, frolicking in waist-deep water, begging us to watch them show off.

"What's going on?" I asked my wife. "Something magic in the water?"

"I don't think it's the water," she said, digging her toes into the warm white sand. "I think it's the beach."

Indeed. Instead of the mud and sharp stones at our pond, this was a lakeside sandbox that softened spills and encouraged kids to linger in the water. I ordered some cheap sand for our place, and it transformed the pond all right—into a cocoa brown silt pit. The pond clouded over with remnants of mud from the unwashed "bank-run" sand I'd bought. After the silt settled, a bloom of thick algae kicked in. Fortunately, the kids didn't mind: They had their own user-friendly mud puddle. And I had taken my first awkward step as a novice beach builder. As I discovered, there's more to beach building than a truckload of sand. But not much more.

Beach Building

Ironically, the soil conditions that lend themselves to a good pond don't offer the best conditions for a bathing beach. To build a pond, you want soil that's rich in clay, which may be stony, hard, muddy, or all the above. For swimming and wading, however, you'd like something easy on the feet—which means sand. Sand is not usually present in a good pond because sand doesn't hold water. (The water drains off, and you're left with a dry beach.) So if you're building or improving a pond, and you want a decent beach, you'll have to make it yourself.

KENYON CONSTRUCTION CO.

If you own waterfront property on a public lake or pond, be sure to check with town officials about the legality of adding sand to your beach. In some areas, concerns about introducing nuisance weeds and algae have prompted officials to prohibit it.

If you're building a pond from scratch, plan the beach area before the contractor does his final grading. The majority of pond beaches I've seen turn up at a point on the shore nearest the access path. This may be convenient, but it may not represent the best beach location. Besides good access, other siting considerations are water depth, shore slope, availability of shade, and dangerous obstacles. Make your beach in the right place, however, and the path will come to meet it.

A beach should be child-friendly, which means a gradual drop-off. A slope of 4:1 extending 10 or 20 feet into the water before sloping down at a steeper angle creates plenty of safe territory for wading and swimming lessons. It's equally pleasant for the elderly. Define a shallow wading area by using rope and buoys, which will give children a safe boundary.

The slope of the shore at water's edge is also important. Setting up a beach on a steep embankment not only limits usage, but also results in sand quickly eroding into the water. Try to find or design a place with as much gently sloping terrain above the waterline as below it. This may mean locating the beach beyond the closest point to your access, but it's worth the walk.

Shade trees near the beach make it easier to protect children and yourself from sunburn, so don't cut a shade tree from the beach site unless it threatens the integrity of a dam or will drop too many leaves into the water. In lieu of natural shade, you can always provide an umbrella or cabana. Picnic tables, barbecue pits, swing sets, and slides may also be welcome additions to a beach. Naturally you don't want to site a beach near anything dangerous. Avoid submerged rocks, mooring anchors, spillways, and electrical wiring.

Once you've got the beach sited, it's time for construction. When digging a new pond, have your contractor carve out an area slightly lower than the existing grade to accommodate the sand. Until recently, many contractors chiseled out and filled with sand a bench 2 or 3 feet deep, knowing that otherwise the soil below would quickly pump up into the sand and displace it. But now, with the introduction of new construction fabrics, it's possible to scoop out a shallower base, line it, use less sand, and keep the soils separate. A subbase 6 inches below grade should suffice. Once that has been excavated, lay down a geotextile drainage fabric over the ground. This fabric consists of a durable porous cloth, often manufactured with woven polyethylene fibers that are UV resistant. The fabric allows water to seep through without clogging, and prevents the sand from mixing with the soil below. The fabric also functions somewhat like a truss rafter, distributing weight so that stepping on the sand doesn't create permanent footprint craters. Geotextile fabrics are available in a variety of materials and costs, although nothing fancy is required for a beach underlayment. One commonly used material is Mirafi septic filter fabric, available at building-supply houses in 3- by 300-foot rolls that cost about 25 cents per square foot.

Beach size depends on your ambitions and budget, but it shouldn't take more than a 20- by 20-foot spread of sand to keep a family happy. In estimating the size of your beach, remember that the submerged area you cover with sand will be mulched against aquatic weeds and algae. In some alga-plagued ponds, the beach may be the only decent place for swimming.

If you're installing a beach at an existing pond, you'll achieve the best result by doing the work in the dry, which means dropping the water level (with a pump, garden hose siphon, or by opening the drain, if you have one). When the beach area is exposed, prepare the subbase as outlined above, laying sand over the geotextile fabric and letting the pond fill again. If you don't want to bother lowering the water, you can lay down the fabric and dump the sand on top. It won't be as neat, but it should work.

When it comes to buying sand, there's little advantage in cutting corners on quality. The truckload of "bank-run" sand I bought from a local gravel pit saved me about $25, but it contaminated the pond. Unless you're planning to cover a huge area, masonry sand is the best choice. Check your local concrete supplier; sand is usually available there. Masonry sand is washed, finely screened, and shouldn't cause turbidity or algae. And because it's lighter in color than cheaper grades, it's cooler in summer. In my neighborhood, masonry sand costs $15 a ton delivered. To estimate your sand costs, multiply the dimensions of your beach (length × width × depth) and divide by 27 to get cubic yards. It takes roughly 1⅓ tons to fill a cubic yard (and order your sand during dry weather to avoid paying for rainwater). For example, sand for a 20- by 20-foot beach 6 inches deep will weigh 7.4 tons. At $15 a ton delivered, that's about $110. Add to that another $100 for the fabric, and perhaps something for the contractor's time, and you

EARTH PONDS VIDEO

may have to spend $300 or so on the beach. The more you do yourself, of course, the more you save.

Whatever you do, don't try making a midnight run on the village sand pit. Road sand is often mixed with salt. It's great for melting highway ice and rusting out cars, but not so good for fish.

Floating through Summer

A couple of years ago, a friend asked for help installing a raft to serve as a swimming and diving platform at his new lakeside house. It was a used raft that he'd managed to scavenge from a girls' camp at the opposite end of the lake. The plan was to go over to the camp in his motorboat and tow the raft to its new home.

It was late August; the camp had closed. We found the raft beached on the sand in two sections, each measuring 5 feet by 10 feet. Getting it across the lake wasn't quite the lark I'd anticipated. We had planned to drag the sections into the water, but they wouldn't budge. Over the years, the polystyrene floats had absorbed water, and under the peeling paint the wood was punky and waterlogged. Eventually, using some sections of pipe for rollers, we were able to pull the raft into the lake. It rode precariously low but miraculously didn't sink.

We fastened the two sections together, tied on a towline, and began the trip back to my friend's house. The raft was so low in the water that I had to ride on the back end to keep the front from nosing under. Slinking across the lake, watching paint flake off into the water, I began to have misgivings about my friend's bargain.

In the fall, after it had been installed at the end of a short pier, the raft was discovered by a family of muskrats, which made a home in the polystyrene. They chewed large holes in the orange billets, spreading debris across the water like a bloom of red tide, and the raft settled lower and lower.

When it occurred to me to build a raft for my own pond last summer, I recalled that trip across the lake and hesitated, reluctant to expose myself to similar problems. I'd already had some experience building a low-budget pier for my pond, rolling a fat hemlock log into the water and spanning the distance to shore with 2-by-6 planks. It made a nice place for sunbathing, but it stuck out into the pond far enough to detour skaters and snag hockey pucks, and after three or four years it started to rot. I hauled it out, let it dry, and burned it. Good thing, too, because by then I had a young daughter who couldn't swim, and I didn't want her wandering out on the pier and falling into water over her head.

I'd also looked into the advantages of rolling docks (see p. 84). These wheel-mounted mobile piers can be launched and retrieved at will, getting around the problem of obstructing skaters but not the danger posed to curious kids who can't swim.

What was left? I liked the idea of an isolated raft anchored offshore, beyond the reach of children. It could be pulled out of the water in the fall, so it wouldn't bother skaters. And it would offer shade and protection for the trout that live in our pond.

The pond is roughly circular, about 90 feet across and 8 feet deep in the middle. High on a sidehill, it mirrors the surrounding landscape, including a bank of lupines, a blueberry hedge, woods, and distant hills. Along the western shore, the sky comes right down to the water. It's attractive in a natural way, and I didn't want to compromise that. I decided to keep the raft small, so it wouldn't appear out of scale, and to use materials that would blend into the scene.

I began with a search for flotation devices. Having seen the limitations of ordinary polystyrene, I looked for alternatives. I recalled seeing large blue plastic barrels for sale at a local hardware store. They turned out to be used fruit-concentrate containers. Because of their durability and low price (about $10 each), they are popular hereabouts for storing water and collecting maple sap. Would they make good floats?

I consulted a local distributor, who told me that some people do, indeed, use the barrels as floats. But when he described the setup—roped-in barrels and a high-riding platform—I envisioned an aquatic seesaw. Considering that I would be hauling my raft in and out of the water, I also anticipated punctures and leaks.

Eventually, my search for floats led me to Bill Koelbel at Dock Hardware and Float Distributors in Geneva, New York. Dock Hardware is a distributor for Follansbee Dock Systems, a large manufacturer of flotation products, including the Series 2 Float Drum, which consists of a durable polyethylene shell molded around a polystyrene core. This type of float is impervious to animals and won't get waterlogged. In the unlikely event of a puncture, the float remains buoyant, and the holes can be patched later. Priced at $59.95, this float wasn't the least-expensive choice, but it looked like the best alternative for my small raft.

When I told Koelbel that I thought a 6- by 6-foot raft would fit my pond best, he advised me not to build one that small. "If you have kids, they'll start rocking the raft, and you don't want it tipping over on them," he pointed out. He suggested 8 by 8—64 square feet—as the minimum size.

As it happens, Follansbee offers an 8- by 8-foot raft kit, including floats, frame, deck, and hardware, for $549.95 plus freight charges. But that kit features a steel frame and plywood deck covered with carpeting, which were not what I wanted for my pond. So I decided to build my own raft, using floats and hardware from Follansbee. This decision saved me about $140 in shipping charges.

The hardware included inside and outside corner braces and washer plates, protected by a PVC coating suitable for fresh or salt water, as well as galvanized carriage bolts and lag bolts. When the hardware arrived, I was surprised to find that the PVC coating was an attractive, enamel-like blue.

My plan for the raft called for a frame made from seven 8-foot 2-by-6s covered with 1-by-6 decking. Koelbel suggested using pressure-treated pine, the choice of most builders for durable outdoor structures. Manufacturers claim that the chemical used in pressure-

A Raft of Pleasures

With an electric circular saw and drill, crescent wrench, screwdriver, measuring tape, and framing square, you should be able to build this floating raft in one or two afternoons. The right hardware makes the raft a snap to assemble. There is a flange around the top of each float, and lag bolts inserted through holes in the flanges attach the floats to the underside of the frame. The removable board in the deck provides access to the anchor line. Using decay-resistant cedar will ensure longevity without the toxic effects of chemically treated lumber.

Materials

Follansbee Floats and Hardware

Floats (FFD-S2): 4
Outside corner angle (LWD-E): 4
Inside corner brace (LWD-IN): 4
Angle (LWD-A): 6
Washer plate (LWD-W): 12
Carriage bolt (3⁄8- x 2½-inch), washer, and nut (F-CB38): 40
3⁄8-inch by 2-inch lag bolt with flat washer (F-LB2H): 24

Lumber (cedar or redwood)

Seven 8-foot 2-x-6s
Eighteen 8-foot 1-x-6s

Other Hardware

2½-inch decking screws (galvanized or rosin-coated), about 3 pounds
Galvanized screw eye for anchor
Ladder

To find a Follansbee distributor near you, contact:

Follansbee Dock Systems
PO Box 610
Follansbee, WV 26037
1-800-223-3444

treated wood—copper chromated arsenate—is locked into the wood cells and will not leach into the environment, but I still didn't want to use it near the water. And the idea of bare skin—my kids' especially—in contact with arsenic-soaked wood wasn't appealing. Other rot-resistant chemicals can be used to extend the life of wood, including creosote and pentachlorophenol, but the same objections apply. The way I figured it, why take any changes with a pristine water supply and the health of children?

I needed a naturally rot-resistant wood. The question was, Which species? I thought of using tamarack (American larch), which is moderately rot-resistant, but couldn't find any at local sawmills or lumberyards. None of the local species that were available seemed suitable. Redwood is often used for outdoor decking and might make a handsome float, but it wasn't generally available at local lumberyards either. Western red cedar seems to have replaced redwood as the most common untreated decking material here in Vermont, and I've seen it used almost without exception for docks around Georgian Bay, Ontario, where the coves and islands are dotted with waterfront cottages. (Unlike us, the Canadians seem to have resisted the lure of pressure-treated wood, especially near the water.) Untreated western red cedar is reputed to last 20 to 30 years when used as decking.

While I was checking out prices for western red cedar, I discovered another variety of cedar that seemed even better for a small raft. Port Orford cedar is harvested from a narrow band of coastal forest in northern

California and southern Oregon. Its tight grain makes it less prone to splintering, and it is sold in smoothly finished 8-foot beams and boards, perfect for my raft. Examining a stack of decking, I found the boards to be mostly clear, with a few tight knots and a nice gingery fragrance. The price of Port Orford cedar at a nearby lumberyard was higher than that of western red cedar—$7.50 for an 8-foot length of 6-inch decking, compared to $5.20—but it was well worth the added cost, I thought.

Building the raft frame requires drilling forty ½-inch holes through the 2-inch cedar, so I recommend doing it close to the house where you can use an electric drill. Then you can disassemble the frame and carry the pieces down to the pond for reassembly.

Start by cutting the 2-by-6 frame pieces to length. Since the finished structure will be 8 feet square, two 2-by-6s will be a full 8 feet, while the balance of five will each be 3 inches shorter.

Drill the holes for the corner braces first, starting from the outside of the frame. Be careful to hold the drill perpendicular to the wood so the holes will line up correctly for the inside corner braces. Bolt the frame together at the corners and make certain that it's square.

Position the crosspieces inside the frame on 2-foot centers and drill the holes for their braces. Check to make sure that everything bolts together properly. Then, after you number the 2-by-6s so that you can put the frame back together correctly, you can disassemble it and move it down to the water.

This is a good place to mention a construction technique for raft and dock projects on difficult terrain. If you happen to live in an area where the water freezes thick enough in winter, build your raft or any other floating dock on ice. Come spring, the finished dock will launch itself. (Don't forget to attach an anchor line.) This is a popular building method on uneven shoreland, or wherever construction space is limited.

Put the frame back together next to the pond, so that after the floats are attached you can launch it easily. There is a flange around the top of each float, with holes for the lag bolts that will fasten it to the frame. Arrange the floats upside down at the corners of the raft and screw them in place with 2½-inch lag bolts and washers.

Flip the frame over into the water. (Enlist a friend to help you lift it if necessary.) Grab it before it floats away and pull one end back up on shore to keep it stable while you lay down the decking. A battery-powered drill will come in handy here, as I recommend predrilling the holes for screws to prevent splitting the cedar. Put in two screws at each point where the decking overlaps a frame piece.

As I laid down the boards, I squared them up on one side of the frame, letting the ends of the boards extend beyond the frame by 1½ inches. Later, using a handsaw, I squared off the ends on the opposite side. I spaced the boards about ½ inch apart to allow for swelling and so rainwater could drain through.

After covering about a third of the deck, check the fit of the remaining boards. I found it necessary to rip a couple of boards down to 3 inches wide so that the last board would wind up flush with the frame. Sand the edges of any ripped boards to avoid splinters.

When you get to the middle of the deck, cut a 2-foot section out of the next board. Measure carefully so that the cut-out section will rest on two of the cross-pieces in the frame. Lay the other two pieces of that board down and screw them in place. The cut-out section now provides a removable hatch through which you can reach an anchor line attached to the frame. This will come in handy in the fall when you want to beach the float without having to swim underneath to untie the line.

I screwed a heavy-duty galvanized screw eye into the frame underneath the hatch. Tying the anchor here rather than at a corner eliminates the risk of diving headfirst into the line. For a larger, rougher body of water, I might use a chain for the anchor, but for my small pond I chose a ½-inch polyprophylene line. An old tractor gear serves as the anchor.

By the time I finished the raft, I'd invested $694 in materials and about 10 hours of labor. A more accomplished carpenter could have done it quicker, and a more frugal builder could have done it for less. Opting to use common inside corner angles for the frame connections, less expensive nuts and bolts, and cheaper lumber would save from $50 to $100. As I mentioned before, I've seen other materials used for flotation (discarded oil barrels were popular at one time) and there's no harm in checking out your local hardware supplier in search of a bargain, or nearby ponds for design ideas; but the way I think about it, my raft is really a kind of boat, and I like it being absolutely seaworthy.

When it came time to launch the raft, I gave it a shove and watched it sail across the pond. Then I swam out and climbed aboard. It seemed surprisingly stable, considering its size. I chose a sunny, slightly off-center mooring in water deep enough for diving and dropped the anchor. Later, looking down at the pond from the house, I found I needn't have been concerned about cluttering up the scenery. The raft looked good.

But it still wasn't quite finished. My daughter Johanna, who was just learning to swim, couldn't get onto the raft without a boost. I spent another $40 for an inexpensive boat ladder and drilled a couple of holes in the deck to attach it. It's adequate, although it doesn't hang quite straight, and it tends to wobble around. I plan to replace it with a more expensive (about $100) rigid model that I saw in a marine-supply catalog. You can get ladders with release mechanisms that let you remove them when you beach the raft for the winter.

Since its launch, the raft has clearly enhanced our use of the pond. It's a place to swim to and goof around on, and for the first time, it gives us a deep-water diving platform. It's especially magnetic for Johanna, giving her the courage to take longer swims, knowing there's a place to catch her breath before the swim back. And last winter we discovered an unanticipated use for the raft: Beached at the edge of the pond, it makes a handy skaters' bench.

Finally, as someone who designs ponds for a living,

Opposite: *This homemade pusher moves more snow than a conventional shovel, and it's easier to maneuver using two hands. This one was built with a discarded storm window frame and a 3½-foot length of 1-by-6 lumber.*

I've found an answer for all of my clients who insist on having an island. I'm generally not in favor of islands in constructed ponds because of the loss of water volume, the increased potential for weeds and algae, and the higher construction cost. (Islands, however, are useful for creating habitat for waterfowl; see Attracting Waterfowl, pages 120–26.) A raft offers many of the advantages of an island without the drawbacks. Besides, you can't haul an island out of the water in autumn to clear the way for the winter's hockey games.

A Rink Master's Primer

Skating Ponds

Sean Mullen's pond lies in a hollow at the end of a narrow gravel road in Orange County, Vermont. In winter, the road weaves between snowbanks past a couple of houses and a hunting camp before the ¼-acre sheet of black ice swings into view. Over the past half-dozen winters, the Mullen pond has become a magnet for neighborhood skaters. On most Sundays at about 2 in the afternoon, the air echoes with the clatter of shovels on the rink. A skater slides the goals into place. Then the players toss their hockey sticks into a pile on the ice, and Mullen divides the sticks into two clumps to choose the teams. Another game of Sunday shinny gets under way.

"It started when we had a couple of years without snow," Mullen recalls. "A lot of people around here got frustrated because they couldn't ski. I made some calls, organized a game, and all kinds of people showed up. I was surprised at how many did. There wasn't a lot of snow that year, so it was easy to keep the pond clear. The games became something of a tradition after that."

Winters without snow haven't become as much of a tradition, so Mullen had to get into the ice-clearing business. He receives a good deal of assistance from other skaters, including a friend with a plow, who helps clear snow after the ice thickens enough to hold a truck. But most of the work is up to Mullen and his wife, Julie.

A snowfall of a half foot or so means three to four hours of clearing for Mullen, using his tracked 5-horsepower, 22-inch snowblower. The blower leaves a residue of snow, so a couple of homemade, handheld pushers with 3-foot blades come in handy to polish off the surface. The Mullens also use steel chippers to shave ice bumps and plane off rough crust. When cracks or frozen slush mar the surface, the Mullens flood the pond and resurface the ice with a portable pump. As the season progresses, the snowbanks around the pond harden and help keep the hockey puck in play.

Skating ponds like the Mullens' have always been popular in the North Country, but there's been a steady increase in the number of neighborhood rinks since snowblowers and lawn tractors have made it possible to improvise a Zamboni in your own backyard. Still, it's a slippery and sometimes scary path to the mastery of rinkmanship, as anyone who's ever heard the thunder of cracking ice underfoot knows. With luck, someone knowledgeable in rink maintenance lives nearby, happy to pass along his expertise. But many pond owners learn the techniques of ice clearing and resurfacing during long, cold hours of on-the-job training.

It snows. You begin to clear the rink. But where do you put the snow? It's tempting to keep the cleared area small—perhaps just enough space for some figure skating; if a larger rink for hockey will be needed later, maybe let the more ambitious clearing wait. But it doesn't work that way. Snow piled on the ice bonds to the surface, settles, and hardens. After a few days, it is difficult—if not impossible—to remove. Meanwhile, perhaps more snow has fallen. The snowbank around the rink perimeter grows. It snows again. If you're shoveling by hand or using a tractor with a plow blade, open ice shrinks as the new snow piles up against the banks. A snowblower can maintain a cleared space only as long as the banks remain low enough to permit the snow to be blown over the top. In a winter with a lot of snow, the skating surface can disappear.

The cardinal rule in maintaining a skating rink is to begin by clearing as large a space as you can manage. If it's feasible to remove the snow from the ice completely, all the better. Not only will a heavy snow load bend the ice and cause cracking, but also ice under a thick layer of snow is insulated and tends to warm up, melt, and seep on the rink. If the snow can't be moved off-ice, a good rule of thumb is to push the rink perimeter back 20 feet beyond the area you want to keep clear. That provides plenty of space for subsequent snow removal.

In determining the rink size, it's important not to make too much work for yourself. If you're clearing by hand and can count on fellow skaters for help, you might be able to maintain a rink large enough for a hockey game. A full-sized rink is 85 feet by 200 feet, but a 60- by 150-foot rink provides enough space for play. Figure-skating rinks can be smaller. My own pond is about 45 by 90 feet. That's too small for hockey, but it's ample for general skating.

The problem is that clearing a rink of any size gets old pretty fast, especially when a fresh snowstorm blows in on the heels of a big clearing job. That's when the snowblowers, tractors, and plowing trucks come in—and sometimes go through.

Before beginning any kind of mechanical clearing, it's essential to know if the ice is strong enough to support the load. In general, 2 inches of ice is considered safe for one person, 4 inches for a group of up to a dozen people, 6 inches for a skimobile or snowblower, and 10 to 12 inches for a truck with a plow. But the strength of the ice depends on quality as well as thickness. New, clear ice may not cover a body of water uniformly, especially over springs and near inlets and outlets. Thicker midwinter ice tends to be more uniform, and 12 inches will support large groups of people and plowing equipment. Yet in spring, warm winds and sun can weaken ice that is more than a foot thick, making it extremely hazardous. Ice will also be weakened by prolonged weight in one spot, as well as by "resonance waves" produced by a moving vehicle. In other words, ice is complicated stuff, and thickness should not be considered the only criterion for safety.

In case of a breakthrough, one of the best rescue devices is a light ladder with a strong line attached to one end. The ladder can be shoved out to the person in the water, then hauled in. The ladder helps distribute weight over a large area. A ring buoy on a rope or even an inflated inner tube can also be used. For self-rescue, iceboaters and others who may be alone on the ice often carry a pair of awls to help pull themselves out. At the very least, a skater ought to carry a knife for the same purpose. Anyone driving a plow truck on ice should make sure the door opens easily and should keep a window open.

As the ice thickens at the start of the skating season, first skaters and then snow-removal equipment can be supported. The lightest machine is a snowblower, so it's the safest for early-season work. Because of its light weight and ease of operation, the snowblower is perhaps the favorite pond-clearing device. A 5-horsepower blower with a 22-inch cut weighs less than 300 pounds. A 36-inch, 11-horsepower blower weighs about 350 pounds. Experienced snow removers favor cuts of 32 inches or longer to reduce clearing time. It may not take long to clear a path between the house and the garage with a small machine, but try opening up a ¼-acre pond some subzero afternoon, and you'll appreciate the extra inches you gain on each pass with a larger snowblower. Besides, the bigger the blower, the farther it throws the snow.

Sean Mullen begins a snow-blowing operation with a pass down the middle of the rink and then works his way out to the edges. "Powder snow will throw about 20 feet; wet snow is like lead," he observes. "One time last year, when it was about 32 degrees, I used the blower to get the snow into windrows, and then people used pushers to move the snow off the rink. I don't think I could have done it with the blower alone."

Pond owners looking for quicker clearing favor small, lawn-type riding mowers or tractors or trucks equipped with a plow blade. A two- or three-hour snowblower job can be handled by a plow in half an hour. But because of the plowing rig's extra weight, it may be unsafe to bring a truck or tractor on the ice as early as you could a snowblower. And there are many winters when you can't wait for thick ice to begin clearing operations. If the first snows aren't removed promptly, the skating surface may remain buried. Besides, a plow may not be able to push heavy snow without using chains, which would mar the ice.

Whatever the means of snow removal, after the initial clearing a residue of snow remains to be swept or scraped away. One of the best tools for this is a homemade pusher incorporating a 3-foot plywood blade with a metal edge and a 7-foot handle. I find that a double handle works even better. In the hands of a couple of good skaters, this type of scraper can cleanly polish off a rink in short order, and it can be used every hour or so during hockey games. Clean ice not only means a faster puck, but it also means the cracks stay visible. A skater catching a blade in a crack at high speed can lose his footing and maybe his senses.

Cracks routinely mar the surface throughout the skating season. They are triggered by expansion and contraction of the ice, fluctuations in water level, and deflection caused by the weight of accumulated snow. It is possible to fill cracks with water and allow it to freeze, but the new ice may pop out of the fissures as it expands. A water-and-snow mixture seems to work better, with snow packed into the crevice and water added. Flooding may be required to fix a badly cracked surface or one roughed up by frozen wet snow.

Black ice forms on a pond or lake when the surface freezes without incorporating any snow in the ice. Skating connoisseurs consider this the crème de la

Just because you don't have a pond doesn't mean you can't skate. This field has been transformed into a skating rink by laying out a plastic membrane and then flooding it during cold weather. Come summer, your ice pond disappears and you can start up the mower again.

Many legendary figure skaters and hockey stars cut their teeth on pond ice, and despite the advent of artificial rinks, outdoor skating has lost none of its magic—in fact snow blowers and portable pumps make it easier than ever to groom pond ice for nice skating.

crème of ice. Black ice is usually a short-lived phenomenon at the beginning of the skating season, mutating into a blue-white surface as winter progresses. But even a full season of black ice isn't flawless. Black ice is exceptionally strong, but it becomes brittle with deep cold and fractures readily. Again, flooding is the remedy.

The cardinal rule for flooding is that too little water is better than too much. It's important to build up the new surface with a thin veneer of ice. The idea is to "grow" the ice upward from the old surface, rather than create another pool that freezes from the top down. Too much flooding often creates pockets of water or air trapped between the ice layers. The best temperature for flooding is a bit below freezing—in the low 20s. If temperatures are too low, the ice freezes unevenly.

Sometimes a pebbled effect is created when splashing water freezes during extremely cold weather. And subzero temperatures make the job miserable.

The volume of water required for flooding is usually about 1,500 gallons per ¼ acre. That's enough to build up ⅛ to ¼ inch of new ice. The water may come from the pond itself, a nearby stream, or the household water supply. Given a generous flow of water through the pond, it's simple enough to cut a hole in the ice and use a pump. Naturally, the hole should be cut outside the rink area. A pump with a 2-inch outlet is generally sufficient to do the job, and reducing the hose to 1¼ inches makes the volume of water more manageable. The best strategy is to begin at one end of the rink and work backward, so you won't be walking on the new surface.

Sometimes, if you pump too much water from the pond, the ice sags and cracks. This is not because of the weight of the water on top of the surface; rather, it's because of the loss of buoyancy from underneath. Then it's time to find a new source of water. If you use household water, make sure that the water system's capacity is equal to the volume needed for flooding. One advantage of household water is that it can be applied warm. Indoor skating rinks are often resurfaced with warm water, which creates exceptionally smooth ice because the water melts the old surface before it freezes. You wouldn't want to heat up enough water to flood ¼ acre, but it takes only a few hundred gallons to put a slick new surface on my ⅛-acre figure-skating rink.

Cracked ice is not the only reason for flooding a rink. "Wet snow means you have to flood," Mullen says, because the snow bonds to the surface of the ice and makes it rough. Short of a complete resurfacing, flooding is also good for touch-up work in small patches, and it helps to level uneven ice. Flooding even makes it possible to have a skating rink when you don't have a pond.

Field Hockey

Creating a flooded rink is like building a pond every year. There's a lot of preliminary site preparation involved, and a delicate balancing act with the weather. It's important to select or create a stretch of flat terrain; seal the rink with ice, packed snow, or a waterproof liner; and then build up and maintain the ice by flooding, spraying, scraping, and clearing. Snowblowers and portable pumps help to make it happen, but the primary ingredients are human initiative and labor. It takes at least one true zealot to keep the ice. Not long ago, my town had a skating rink that was a magnet for hockey players and figure skaters and once provided the inspiration for a nostalgic *New Yorker* magazine cover. Now it's a snow-covered potato patch. The rink master moved to Alaska, and the skating went with him.

Level ground is essential for good skating-rink construction, particularly if an earth base will be used. Vermont's Division of Recreation suggests a maximum fall of 1 inch per 100 feet, while conceding that it is possible to make ice on surfaces that decline as much as 18 inches per 100 feet, if the temperature is zero or below. Naturally, the more uneven the surface, the more water required.

You can use a hand level or transit to determine the slope of the land. People who put their first rink on a slope quickly learn that water won't tilt. Some try to overcome this problem by using a high curb at the low end. Occasionally it works; mostly it doesn't. Leaks and difficulty in layering ice at the deep end are frequent problems. So leveling the site is a top priority. Leveling can be done by hand for a small rink, using a shovel and rake; you'll need a tractor or bulldozer for a larger rink.

Perhaps the greatest obstacle to rink construction is water seepage. Porous soil allows water to drain away, making it difficult to establish a solid base of ice. It's important to find soil with enough clay content to hold the water while it freezes. An area with a cover of mowed grass holds water better than does raw earth. Clip the grass short and rake it before flooding or spraying; fewer decaying leaves will float up in the ice to ruin the surface.

Keep snow off the rink area during early winter to allow the ground to freeze. Frost to a depth of 3 to 6 inches is essential for a good base. It may help to spray the rink and allow the moisture to seep into the ground and freeze. Some rink builders have had luck with a base of tamped-down snow, using a four-wheel-drive vehicle for packing.

One obvious way to avoid the whole problem of seepage is to use a waterproof liner. The liner may be a permanent cover, such as asphalt, or a temporary one of plastic. The liner can also help overcome problems with slope.

Alleyne Howell takes care of the Vershire, Vermont, skating rink. He says he does it because he loves to skate, and indeed he must, because over the past three years he has faced a combination of natural obstacles and bureaucratic resistance that would have undone a less enthusiastic soul. When the town built a playing field, Howell saw the opportunity to enhance it with a winter skating rink, and in fact a group of local kids had begun to level the ground in preparation for the rink. But the village elders objected, fearing that a skating rink in the middle of town would attract rowdies and vandals.

"First they were nervous about teens using it," Howell recalls, "and then they feared it wouldn't be proper on the state-funded playing field. But as it turned out, a skating rink is a legitimate winter use of a playing field." Howell circulated a petition and won overwhelming support for the rink. "Democracy blew them away," he says.

But democracy doesn't blow away snow, so Howell has to use a truck. "The worst part is plowing after a big storm," he says, explaining that the ice makes steering rather dicey. The advantage is that plowing is usually quick, and he doesn't have to worry about his truck breaking through and sinking.

"This is a low-tech operation. After the ground is frozen, I pack the first big snowfall with my jeep, running back and forth over it. That's better than plowing it off because it has a white surface that reflects the sun and stays cold. After Christmas, I spray the rink to get a watertight surface, and then I flood it."

Howell uses a 3-horsepower portable gas pump to draw water from a nearby stream. He builds up the surface in layers ¼ to ½ inch thick. Total thickness is about 3 to 4 inches. "The rink isn't perfectly level, so sometimes I'll get a frozen ripple effect on the downhill end," Howell says. "Eventually, we're hoping to build a paved basketball court that will double as a rink in winter."

While pavement covered with a sealant is unquestionably the ideal base for a flooded rink, plastic sheeting is an effective and economical alternative, especially for a relatively small backyard rink. Tom MacMillan uses plastic for his 56- by 24-foot figure-skating rink in Lebanon, New Hampshire. The plastic prevents seepage and enables him to correct for a slope of 4 inches over the length of the rink. MacMillan uses two sheets of construction-grade plastic overlapping a foot or two, with the uphill sheet on top. The seam is sealed with duct tape.

MacMillan's rink is surrounded by a curb of 2-by-4s supported by stakes driven into the ground. He runs the plastic up over the 2-by-4s, then staples strips of cardboard over the plastic to secure the edge. The plastic is good only for one season, but it doesn't cost much. MacMillan figures he spent only about $35 on materials for his rink last winter, including plastic and lumber. Flooding the rink probably added $35 to his water bill, "but I don't consider that an exorbitant price to pay for having a rink outside my door," he says.

Building up the ice in a flooded rink is a fine art. Spraying is the most reliable method for layering ice without creating air pockets and uneven areas. The Vermont Division of Recreation recommends the following procedure:

Start at the end of the rink farthest from the water supply, walking backward to the opposite end. Work across the rink, back and forth, moving fast enough to match water to water; that is, each pass across the rink should overlap the previous pass before the water has frozen. Hold the nozzle of the hose up, rather than parallel or downward. Don't drag the hose on new ice or allow it to lie on the ice in one spot too long. Little or no water should be standing on the rink when each layer is finished. Scrape off any bumps and grass blades and fill in any holes before applying another layer. The next layer should be applied when the surface is frozen but still tacky, like fresh paint. Continue to build up layers until you have 3 or more inches of ice.

The volume of water required to establish a skating surface will vary with the thickness of the ice and the size of the rink. Three inches of water on a rink 100 by 75 feet adds up to approximately 14,000 gallons. That's enough to overdraw the supply on many private household water systems, which helps to explain why many flooded rinks are community affairs tended by the local fire department.

Tom MacMillan's modest backyard rink requires only 2,500 gallons of water and provides a whole winter's entertainment. After his workday is over, he likes to come home, put on his Walkman, and practice his spins in the light of the Coleman lantern that hangs on a ladder beside the rink.

"I don't have to drive to the nearest indoor rink and pay to get in; I don't have to listen to music I don't like; I don't bump into any crowds," he says. He also enjoys the safety of ice that won't break through. He can't swim.

From Hay Rake to Rolling Dock

Ninety percent of the pond and lake docks I've encountered are conventional walkways anchored firmly to shore. Some of them stay in the water year-round; others can be disconnected from shore and pulled up on land, usually with the help of more than a few strong backs or a truck. One of the most unusual docks I've run across belongs to a neighbor, Donny Prescott. The shore-bound end of the dock rests on the pond embankment, while the far end stands on a pair of large old wagon wheels submerged in a couple of feet of water. The far end juts out just enough so that the drop into the pond basin is overcome by the height of the wheel axle, and the dock stands level. This is a dock that cleverly gets around most of the liabilities of a permanent installation.

First off, especially in a small pond, where do you site the dock? Close to a shallow shore might be great for kids and sunbathers and skaters lacing up, but what about trout? The shade cast by a dock can be a lifesaver for overheated fish, but it's best in deep water where the trout hang out. The remedy? A dock on wheels that can be rolled around to fit the season and the crop.

Permanently mounting a dock is tricky in ponds where the water level bobs up and down according to runoff and rainfall. A dock over deep water in April may be high and dry come July. On wheels, however, it can be positioned to match the inland tides.

A dock is the perfect place to lash a cage full of fish being fattened for the table. It offers easy access for stock, feeding, and harvest. Cage culture works best in deep water, but come winter, after harvest and nearing time for hockey, who wants a dock in center ice? Better to put the dock on wheels, so it can be in deep one day and beached for safekeeping the next.

Finally, the pond keeper who anticipates touch-up shoreline excavation or dredging would want a dock that could be pulled out of the way during repairs.

Donny told me that he built his rolling dock with a pair of 12-foot, 2- by 6-inch boards for carrying timbers, 1-inch planking, and part of a side delivery hay rake. The old rake was rusting out in the scrap yard alongside Donny's repair shop. After dismantling the rake, he trucked the axle and the wheels to the pond. He rolled the wheels into the water so that the axle set just above water level. Then he mounted the carrying beams over the axle at one end and onshore at the other. After that he nailed on the planking. The length of the axle determines the width of the dock.

I asked Donny for tips on building a rolling dock.

"I'd try to match the height of the wheels with the

depth of the pond where you want to set it," he told me. "The deeper you want to go, the bigger the wheels. Get your axle and wheels first, and remember you can only roll in the water up to the axle. If you want to extend the dock beyond the wheels, you might want to stake down the shore end so it doesn't tip. I think you'll have good luck if you keep a lookout for old farm machinery." Donny didn't mention it, but I'd recommend using rot-resistant cedar or redwood, or perhaps treated lumber to prevent decay. There are, of course, many other options for dock design: docks that float, docks resting on permanent pilings, and modular docks that can be extended piece by piece into the water and then taken apart for winter storage. One of the best ways to check out dock design options is to take a boat ride around a local lake, where each cottage may offer inspiration.

A rolling dock gathers no moss. It can be moved to make way for wintertime skaters and dredging equipment, adjusted to changing water levels, or hauled in for repairs.

Tap Your Pond for Fire Protection

There's a saying in the hills that the fire department is great at saving cellar holes; insurance premiums for backwoods homes reflect that pessimistic attitude. The combination of woodstoves, snow-covered roads, and widely scattered volunteer firefighters makes any insurance underwriter edgy. And winter is not the only dangerous season. Last summer, a squad of local firemen raced up to a blazing house, hooked the hose to the tank truck, and found that somebody had forgotten to load the truck with water. Luckily, there was a pond nearby.

A pond may be a rural homeowner's best fire insurance policy. A general-purpose pond as small as 1/10 acre, 9 feet deep at the dam, holds approximately 100,000 gallons of water. That's more than enough to feed a pump truck all the water necessary to save almost any house or barn, if the truck gets there in time. But to make a homestead even safer, you need an on-site delivery system.

If your pond is sited above your buildings, gravity will deliver the water you need. Indeed, many an old farm was served by a single gravity-feed line that supplied irrigation and livestock water as well as fire protection. Water picks up pressure at roughly ½ pound per vertical foot, so a decent fire stream of 70 pounds of pressure requires at least 140 feed of "head." Of course, it's possible to make do with less.

If your pond is not situated high enough for a gravity-fed water system, you'll need a pump to take advantage of a pond's fire-fighting potential. There's nothing more pathetic than fighting a blaze with a five-minute chemical extinguisher while a pond ripples nearby, untapped. I once fought a brushfire that way, raking firebreaks, digging trenches, glaring in frustration at the pond 100 yards below. Luckily, late in the afternoon, the wind shifted and the fire died. With a pondside pump and a

Water is a vital resource, and with a portable pump it need not be confined to the pond. Pumps can be used for garden irrigation and fire protection, as well as resurfacing skating ice, and for emergency aeration in the event of a fishkill.

hose, I could have doused the fire in minutes and then gone for a swim.

Centrifugal or pressure pumps can deliver more than 100 gallons a minute through 1½-inch hose. Portable models with pull-rope starters—something like a chainsaw engine fitted with plumbing instead of a chain—are ideal for fire fighting. New, one of these two-cycle gasoline pumps costs upward of $400. Hose runs close to $1 a foot, and a plastic fire nozzle costs about $15. But before you buy equipment, check with the local fire department; often you'll find secondhand equipment for sale.

The pump should be set up near the pond in a small shelter, ready to go. Make certain there's always a quart of water or antifreeze on hand for priming, and test-start the pump every month. Keep in mind the basic requirements for a home fire pump: It should deliver a fire stream of at least 100 gallons per minute with pressure at the nozzle of at least 70 pounds.

Next to the pump, a "dry" hydrant is the pond owner's best protection in the event of a fire. A dry hydrant is a freezeproof tap into the pond. It looks like your basic Main Street fireplug, but what you don't see is a pipe going down below frost line and taking a turn into the bottom of the pond. With the help of a pump (usually aboard a fire truck), the hydrant provides instant access to a reservoir much larger than the truck's own water tank. Usually, a dry hydrant is installed during pond construction; you can add one to an existing pond but it's likely to be expensive. New hydrants are expensive, too, but fire departments, which often replace old ones when they change fittings, sometimes have perfectly good secondhand hydrants for sale.

The main considerations in siting a dry hydrant are to make it accessible to fire trucks and to put it near the house. One of my neighbors has a roadside dry hydrant that's located 50 yards from her pond, close by her home. Another has a similar setup, but it's only 20 feet from pond to hydrant. Naturally, the closer the hydrant to the pond, the less the expense for pipe and installation. Keeping the hydrant plowed out in the winter is crucial, and some highway crews will go out of their way to clear one. It's also smart to put a mesh filter on the inlet pipe to keep silt from clogging it. (Some pond keepers shortcut the dry hydrant completely by allowing a disk of Styrofoam to freeze in the ice near shore; the Styrofoam can be punched out for quick access to the water. If the pond is any distance from the road, however, this is impractical.)

A pond equipped with a pump or hydrant will provide fire protection, a little peace of mind, and perhaps even more: You may get lower insurance rates, as long as the underwriter is convinced that you will maintain the system properly. One of my neighbors even had his pond dropped from the tax rolls in exchange for a hydrant that would be available to the fire department.

Irrigation and a Low-Budget Zamboni

One of the excellent aspects of pond ownership is that it opens up potentials beyond the pond, perhaps most significantly garden irrigation. One of the first things I did after building our pond was to put in a new garden.

Our second, it was sited downhill from the pond where I could water it with a gravity siphon hose. That didn't make it any easier to weed, however, and eventually I returned to the original garden, which had better soil and better sun exposure. Whenever necessary, irrigation water came from our well or by hand uphill from the pond. The catch was that during a serious drought I couldn't afford to use much well water on the garden without running us out of drinking water, and lugging it up from the pond Sherpa-fashion got old fast. I remember one summer when the sky seemed to forget how to rain. Nothing grew. That summer half the garden went to weeds. The next summer I got a pump.

To take care of our 50- by 50-foot plot, I decided that a lightweight, portable, gas-powered pump would work best. Portability was important, because on top of using it to water the corn, I wanted to be able to Zamboni the ice in winter and have it on standby for burning brush piles (see Fire Protection, page 85–87). Small two-cycle centrifugal pumps can also provide emergency aeration during a fishkill, clean out a flooded basement, or hose down a house threatened by wildfire (lacking a pond, it helps to have a swimming pool full of water nearby). Mobility was the big attraction; besides, I've never liked the idea of electric lines near water.

Most lawn and garden shops offer portable pumps, and I chose a $300 Echo WP 1000, which is about the size of a chain saw and almost as loud. It starts reliably and delivers up to 27 gallons per minute the 100 or so feet uphill to my garden. Before buying a pump, it's important to measure the distance you need to move water and the total head (vertical distance from water surface to outlet), and make sure the pump is qualified.

During dry weather I connect the pump to a garden sprinkler and run it for about an hour (one tank full), which is enough time to lay down roughly an inch of water (over an area of about 2,500 square feet). Moving around the sprinkler, I can cover the entire garden in four evenings giving the crops their recommended 1-inch weekly allotment, and avoiding an overdose of engine noise (after all, it's called an Echo). Watering after sunset or on cloudy days minimizes evaporation and maximizes efficiency.

I level up the pump on a plywood pallet close to the water and drop the intake in a bucket sunk just offshore, which prevents the pump from sucking up mud. (Centrifugal pumps do not like mud; some larger diaphragm pumps can handle detritus, hence the name trash pumps.) I've learned to take special care not to spill gas when I'm filling the tank, and I store fuel away from the pond, where any accidental spills won't foul the water. The pump is covered with a metal hood when not in use, or put away.

As far as resurfacing the ice in winter, it works best when the temperature is in the low 20s (see Ice Skating, page 80). The tricky part is to keep the priming water in the pump from freezing. It may be necessary to warm up the pump before you use it. It also helps to have the hole in the ice prepared and the hose ready to hook up. All water should be drained out of the pump before winter storage to prevent damage from expanding frozen water.

When a continuous flow of water is required, electric pumps outperform gas. They use less energy and make a lot less racket. They can be used to add or subtract water from a pond, and to circulate the water within to destratify temperatures and boost oxygen. Electric centrifugal pumps are popular for constant duty, and are available from most aquaculture-supply outfits. If you're looking for a demonstration of how a centrifugal pump works, jump into the nearest hot tub. Jacuzzi is one of the largest electric pump manufacturers, for aquaculture as well as hot tubs.

In situations where no commercial AC power is available, smaller 12-volt pumps can be powered by battery or solar cells. You may be able to use hydro ram pumps in some nonelectric situations, where a minimum flow of water already exists. The ram operates by using about 90 percent of the flow to drive the remainder back uphill, above the original source. Wind-powered water pumps are also available (see Resources, page 61).

Raising Fish

Once you've seen trout making rings on a mirror-smooth pond or bass chasing bluegill through the cattails, a pond without fish looks incomplete. Sooner or later most pond owners are going to want to raise fish, for the table or simply the view. After a trip to the nearest hatchery, the hasty ride home with a plastic bag full of panicky fingerlings, and the cascade of fish into the water, here's how to make their upbringing as successful as possible. (Of course, if you want fish in any quantity, or if you have to drive any distance, they'll have to be delivered.)

Warm-Water Fish

Matching the right fish to your pond temperature is the first task. Ponds with consistent summer temperatures of 70 degrees F or higher are usually stocked with warm-water fish: Bass, bluegills, and catfish top the list of favorites. Successful warm-water fish culture depends on a pond that supports a hierarchy of plant and animal life, from the lowliest zooplankton to the bass at the top of the food chain. Prerequisites for warm-water fish ponds include soil of sufficient fertility to support vegetation, shallow areas where vegetation can develop, and good water quality. Ponds as small as 1/10 acre are used, although many biologists recommend a minimum of 1 acre.

Stocking: Decades of experimentation by fisheries biologists and pond owners have resulted in a basic stocking strategy that combines largemouth bass and bluegills, both noted for putting up an exciting fight. Assuming the pond provides a good foundation of natural food (insects, tadpoles, zooplankton, snails, crawfish, minnows, and so on), the bluegills will graze on the natural feed, and the bass will feed on the bluegills and everything else. When it works, it's a productive food pyramid, especially for pond owners who don't want to be involved in fish-feeding programs. However, there's more to it than simply dumping in small fish and waiting for table-sized fish to appear. In

If you live close to a fish hatchery, you may be able to purchase fish and bring them home yourself. At greater distances, hatcheries prefer to deliver the fish to guarantee survival. These trout fry are being sized prior to shipment.

fact, before you put in any fish, be sure the pond isn't already occupied by a population that will upset your plans. Fish that are generally not welcome include crappies, which tend to overwhelm the bass, and bullheads, carp, buffalo, suckers, and green sunfish, which can become dominant and/or cause turbid water. One of the best ways to determine if an existing pond contains unwanted fish is to seine out a sample. (Seine nets are available from most aquatic suppliers.) A 10-foot minnow seine can be pulled through shore water to come up with a fish count. Do this between June and August, to sample the new population before it's big enough to dodge the net. In ponds with an existing population of bass and bluegill, seining should let you know how close you are to the roughly 10:1 ratio of bluegill to bass, and what you need to do to establish the correct balance.

An imbalance of bluegills and bass, or an excess of unwanted species, indicates that the pond may have to be drained to get off to a fresh start. Some biologists recommend using rotenone or synthetic chemicals to poison unwanted fish, but I'd think twice before dumping toxins in my pond, especially if swimming is another of its uses, or if it might be a threat to downstream neighbors. Draining a pond to eliminate unwanted fish has the advantage of also allowing you to do any dredging or repairs that might be necessary (see chapter 2, Maintenance).

Your first decision is how many fish to stock. This will depend on the size of the pond. Acreage recommendations vary from 50 to 100 bass per surface acre, with an accompanying population of 500 to 1,000 bluegill fingerlings.

In ponds being stocked from scratch, some pond owners stock the fish simultaneously; others introduce the bluegills first, in the fall, and then add bass the following spring. By then, the bluegills will be reproducing tasty little ones for the arriving bass. At least one summer of growth is required before fishing should start, although some pond owners wait until the end of the second summer. How many should you fish out? Biologists recommend about 80 pounds of bluegill to 20 pounds of bass. Once the fish reach harvest size, it's important to keep up a fishing regimen that reduces the population by a ratio of about four times as many bluegills as bass. No bass smaller than 12 inches should be taken. Some biologists recommend not taking bass between 12 and 15 inches because at that size they are the most efficient feeders. Unless you can maintain the correct harvest ratio, one of the species will go out of balance and the self-sustaining character of the pond will cease. What often happens is that the bass are fished out first, the bluegills soon take over, and you wind up with a pond full of stunted panfish. If for some reason the bluegills are fished out, the bass will die off, having lost their main food source. And if you don't do any fishing at all, a population of stunted bluegills usually takes over. Fishing records are essential to keep track of the harvest ratio.

In addition to the no-frills bass-and-bluegill mix, pond owners sometimes stock channel catfish, at a rate of about 50 to 100 per surface acre—more if they receive supplemental feed. Although not necessary in a healthy pond where the bass-bluegill mix is correct, supplemental feed can be used for many species. Aquatic suppliers, including *Farm Pond Harvest* magazine, offer feeding devices. Channel cats are not likely to reproduce in ponds; even if they do, the fry won't last long with bass and bluegill around. Redear and hybrid sunfish are also sometimes stocked. For pond owners who don't want to be bothered with a strict fishing routine, bass can be stocked alone. They may not grow as dramatically as they would with a bluegill diet, but they should do well on a diet of crawfish, tadpoles, and minnows. Minnows are sometimes added to a pond just to keep the bass happy.

Cold-Water Fish

Raising fish in cold-water ponds is simpler than farming fish in more temperate climates. For most pond owners it boils down to one variety of fish—trout—and one species—rainbow. The fish are stocked as small fry (4 to 6 inches is a good size) and harvested at between 1 and 2 pounds. A good trout pond should have clean, clear water, with a source of incoming water sufficient to keep the water from becoming stagnant. It helps to have some shade, either from nearby trees or from a dock or raft, to give the fish a place to cool off in summer. Trout also appreciate a deep basin furnished with rocks, where they can seek shelter and cool temperatures.

Cold-water ponds should provide summer temperatures up to but not above 70 degrees F. Trout grow best between 50 and 60 degrees F. Rainbows are usually favored because they will tolerate brief temperatures up to 75 degrees F. Ponds where high temperatures are not a problem will support brook trout, which some people feel has a higher-quality meat. Oxygen is another important factor. Many ponds in the Midwest feature lower-layer temperatures suitable for trout, although oxygen levels may be inadequate due to the high oxygen demand of decaying pondbed organic matter and low light levels that cut off photosynthesis. Trout need at least 5 parts per million of dissolved oxygen to thrive. Trout also require a pH of between 6.5 and 8.5.

EARTH PONDS VIDEO

There are several ways to determine whether your pond will sustain trout. One of the simplest ways is to stock a small amount and see how they do. If they don't survive, you know you've got a problem but you haven't wasted a lot of money. It's also possible to use water-analysis devices to check oxygen levels (see Resources, page 107). Your state extension service may be able to help you, or perhaps a local trout supplier who might then benefit from your business.

Given good temperatures and oxygen levels, trout will do well in ponds as small as 1/10 acre, with average fertility. In such ponds it's possible to raise 100 to 200 pounds per surface acre. A finished trout weighs about a pound, so you'll be stocking roughly one fish for every finished pound; most pond owners add 5 to 10 percent when they stock, figuring on losses due to predators, and so on. Adding supplemental feed can boost that yield as much as tenfold, although oxygen may need to be added through an aeration system. The best trout ponds usually have a source of springwater coming in from a stream or surface vein of water, which helps oxygenate the water. Springwater from the bottom may not include enough oxygen.

Ponds that do not offer cold enough water in summer may sustain trout during a winter growing season. Trout stocked in November and harvested in May or June may gain enough in size to be a worthwhile project. Such ponds are often dedicated entirely to trout, and the grown fish seined out. Smaller amounts of winter trout can be stocked with other species and then fished out by hook and line.

Feeding Fish

In general, feeding fish supplemental food is not necessary if enough natural food is present and the fish are not overstocked. In fact, one of the many advantages of an earth pond is that it supports plant and animal life that sustain fish. In warm-water ponds, the whole point of mixing forage and game fish is to create a self-sustaining habitat. Trout growers, however, are more likely to use supplemental feed. Feeding allows you to stock higher amounts of fish, and to bring them to harvest size quicker. It takes about 1 pound of feed to produce ½ pound of fish. It's important not to overfeed. Feed that isn't cleaned up often winds up adding to the alga problem, and feed should not be offered when temperatures exceed 65 degrees F. You must be careful not to overstock. Be aware, too, that in times of stress (hot weather and low oxygen), a large population of fish is at higher risk of fishkill. Any fish losses, of course, translate into greater financial losses if you've been spending money feeding them. In general, feeding fish requires a higher degree of fish management.

Closed Systems

Fish culture is not limited to ponds. Professional and amateur growers employ closed systems using recirculated water. Tanks include everything from swimming pools (no chlorine, please) to specially designed models with circulation filters. For backyard fish culture, warm-water fish are usually favored, as they grow fast and generally tolerate confined conditions. Catfish, tilapia, and striped bass are usually stocked, although other fish can be grown. Aquatic Eco-Systems' Mini Fish Farm can fit in a 6- by 8-foot area, requires only 10 gallons of water daily to refresh its 400-gallon tank, and will product 50 pounds of fish. The Alternative Aquaculture Association also produces plans for building economical backyard fish tanks.

Predators

Whether you're raising warm- or cold-water fish, predators can wipe out a hard-earned crop overnight. Herons and kingfishers are among the worst offenders, and because they're protected species, thwarting them requires some creativity. Scare-away balloons, whistles, explosives, and even inflatable men are used, as well as netting. Dogs are helpful at keeping edge-feeding herons away, but they don't have much effect on kingfishers. Muskrats and otters can also devastate a fish crop. They are not protected, so they can be trapped or shot (see Muskrats, page 132.)

Cage culture is another way to beat predators. Fish are raised in net cages or cylinders that usually float just beneath the pond surface. The cage protects against predators attacking from the water or the sky. Cage culture also enables growers to raise different species or sizes of fish within the same system, in different cages, without having to worry about interspecies competition or losing fry to larger fish. Once fry reach mature size they can be released into the larger environment, if desired. Cage culture also simplifies harvesting.

Cage culture requires daily feeding and attention, and if not maintained carefully can be lethal to fish. The fish have to be stocked at the correct density. Too many, they're overcrowded and die; too few, they fight and kill each other. Rubbing up against the netting can cause skin damage that leads to mortality, and the surface level location can lead to overheating. It was Jay Huner who alerted me to the problems associated with cage culture, and he concluded, "Without daily care, they can be the most efficient fish killers ever made."

Fee Fishing

For fish farmers using earth ponds, fee fishing can be a way to augment income. In fact, some commercial growers are hoping to arrange fee-fishing operations to generate a significant part of their income. Fee fishing is similar to pick-your-own-vegetable arrangements on truck farms. The farmer supplies the product, the customer harvests it. Successful fee-fishing operations rely on fish that bite. Since most fee fishing happens in the summer, that can be tricky, considering how lazy some fish become on hot afternoons. Fee-fishing proprietors may have to supplement their ponds with cold water or install aeration systems to stimulate fish appetites in summer. Emphasis on morning or evening fishing may be equally helpful. Tables and outdoor grills where customers can turn their catch into a picnic can enhance fee-fishing areas. Some trout ponds are limited to fly-fishing; others may require (and often sell) barbless hooks. Fee fishing is usually paid for by the pound, depending the catch. Hosting a fishing derby cosponsored by a local organization like the Boy Scouts or volunteer fire department is another way to promote fee fishing. Insurance coverage against liability is generally recommended.

Pondscapes: Keep It Simple

When people ask me for suggestions about decorating around a pond I confess to membership in the no-froufrou school of design. A pond is a living sculpture, and the same is true of garden pools. Flowing water, kaleidoscopic reflections, plants, fish, and wildlife are hard to beat. But some folks insist on more. There's a trend in "exterior decorating" to gussy up backyards, ponds, and fish pools with a mishmash of ornamentation from lead cupids to an "artfully" arranged family of plastic ducks. I think many backyards are beginning to resemble a stir-fry of leftovers from Versailles, L.L. Bean, and a John Waters movie set. Hammocks, pink flamingos, cabanas, plastic lawn chairs, Christmas lights, and kerosene torches clutter the shore. The scene looks more like a yard sale than a yard. But to each his own!

A small embellishment or two in the right place can be welcome. It might be something as simple as a pair of Adirondack chairs overlooking the water, a picnic table near a sandy beach, a teak garden bench, perhaps even a garden shed or sauna. And if your decorating also takes care of practical needs, so much the better.

Soon after our kids were born, it became apparent that we needed some shade on the shore to shelter napping babies and a nursing mother. A large beach umbrella inserted in a movable concrete pad filled the bill. Eventually we added a picnic table and a couple of discreet sculptures. A floating raft also contributes a design element (see Floating through Summer, page 70–76). Except for occasionally setting up a camping tent by the water for overnights with the kids, that's it. As far as plantings go, there's a row of blueberries along the edge of the dam, with a plum tree at one end, and a bank of blue-and-white lupines overlooking the water. It adds up to a low-key signature: People as well as wildlife welcome.

Stonework

Stonework is another attractive way to improve a pond. An aerating waterfall cascading down a stone-lined inflow, a retaining wall along shore, or a diving stone set at the water's edge can add aesthetic value, and practical advantages, too. Embankment ponds in particular often benefit from retaining walls along steep upslope shoreland. These walls prevent erosion and create useful terraces. A contractor I often work with distinguishes his ponds with the quality of his stonework. In addition to building top-notch basins, he and his son have a flair for retaining walls and attractive stone arrangements. It's not something you learn overnight. His family has owned a quarry for years, and setting stone comes to him as naturally as jockeying a bulldozer. If you decide to incorporate stonework in your pond project, be sure your contractor has the necessary skills.

KENYON CONSTRUCTION CO.

Gazebos and Bridges

Other interesting landscaping features include gazebos and bridges. Gazebos are available prefab and complete, or you can build one from a variety of plan books. Often quite ornate, they can transform a pond into a Victorian trysting place or a Buddhist temple garden. In addition to being a mood enhancer, a gazebo actually offers some practical benefits: a shaded area for kicking back, entertaining, picnics, children's activities, and putting on skates. Add screening and you can enjoy the pond during mosquito season. I've even seen a gazebo on concrete pilings in the middle of a new pond, linked to shore by a long pier. Too bad the pond never filled up: The gazebo looks like a Jules Verne spaceship marooned in a lunar crater. The moral? If you want to put a gazebo in the water, be sure you've got the water.

Pond styles run the gamut from funky farm watering hole to fancy fish pool, and bridges also span a spectrum of styles. Lay a few stepping-stones in the spill-

COURTESY OF BOW BENDS, INC.

Gazebos offer shade, protection from mosquitoes (if screened), and a place for kids to play and adults to relax.

way, drop a wooden plank across an inflow, erect an arched bridge. In my experience, bridges aren't a high priority among pond owners. In fact, where piped overflows are used, bridges are unnecessary, unless a span across the inflow is desired. When a spillway bridge is required, the simpler the better. For installation, bridges usually require stable footings since the foundation area is likely to be wet. Be sure the bridge is not so low that it traps outgoing debris. Use decay-resistant materials; I prefer natural materials like redwood and cedar to pressure-treated lumber, which has a jaundiced look, besides being saturated with toxic preservatives. New ersatz wood materials are available, fabricated from recycled plastic. A simple arched plank construction, or even a stone slab, can be elegant in a natural setting. Whatever materials you choose, though, remember that bridges intended for heavy vehicles require spanning beams hefty enough to bear their weight.

Saunas and Hot Tubs

For sauna lovers, a dip in the pond is the perfect climax to a hot sweat. The closer together the pond and sauna house, the better. Sauna ponds are also likely to be built close to home, to make access convenient, especially in winter. Being relatively small, the sauna shouldn't be terribly expensive, and it's possible to create something stylish (log cabin; cordwood masonry) without breaking the bank. Saunas range in layout from closet-sized one- or two-person jobs to family saunas of 100 square feet or more. Keep in mind that the bigger you make it, the longer it takes to heat up and stay hot. Saunas are often finished on the inside with cedar or redwood, for both durability and aromatic quality. Saunas can be heated with electric, wood-, or LP stoves. A friend of mine built one on wheels so he could tow it nearer to the house in winter, when the ice made the pond unusable anyway. A sauna on skids could also be towed with relative ease.

Hot tubs are another bathing option. In the same way that a sauna bath benefits from the contrast between hot and cold, it's a delight to dive in a cool pond after a long wallow in a steaming tub. Pondside tubs also make sense because of the proximity of a water supply. If the site lacks electricity, a wood-fired model like the Snorkel fills the bill. The Snorkel incorporates a wood-fired heater inside a large wooden hot tub. When it's filled with broiling bathers, it bears an uncanny resemblance to those old (and now politically incorrect) *New Yorker* cartoons showing hapless missionaries in bubbling cannibal kettles!

Fountains

In some situations—commercial establishments especially—an electric fountain may be an aesthetic necessity. However, it's not a very efficient aerator, and it uses a lot of power. If a dramatic statement is required, though, it'll do the trick. Add lights for nighttime illumination and you turn on a liquid fireworks display.

Stream pools and digger ponds make fine sauna ponds because ice is slow to form in the moving water.

Hydropower

Two hundred years ago, most of the ponds built in this country were designed to power water mills. The art of pond design was closely connected to the development of waterpower. But with the advent of electricity and the needs of a growing population for more energy, pond-powered hydro systems took a backseat to mammoth systems such as the Hoover Dam and Hydro Quebec, as well as fossil fuel and fission generators. Windmills and photovoltaic solar cells further eclipsed small-scale hydropower. I was surprised to discover

The Digger Pond

If you have access to a stream, you may be able to build a small digger pond for wading, sauna bathing, and attracting fish. Because they are less prone to siltation, digger ponds are also useful where streams are used to feed offset ponds or for other water requirements, such as irrigation. The principle is simple. Instead of creating a dam below the pool, which will inevitably fill up with silt, a dam is built upstream, above the pool. As water cascades over the dam, it tends to carve out the basin on its own steam. Hence the term *digger pond.* Since a dam on either side of a pool may interfere with the free flow of a stream (and fish traffic), permission from your state natural resources agency or water resources authority may be required. Many states also regulate construction activity in streams of substantial size.

To build a digger pond, excavate a trench about 2 feet wide and 4 feet deep into the banks, with the base level with the streambed. Lay two sill timbers or logs in the downstream trench and one in the upstream, anchored with ¼-inch reinforcing rods. Site the trenches roughly 4 feet apart. Work should be done during a period of low water flow.

Next, lay 2-inch mesh wire over the sill logs and stream bottom, stapled to the logs. Spike smaller logs to the top of the downstream logs, leaving a midstream gap of 1 or 2 feet. Fasten only the outer ends of the top logs to the sills.

Now cover the wire mesh with brush, and then stones. Anchor the ends with soil and rocks. Next enlarge the notch by cutting back on each log alternately from the center of the spillway until the entire flow of the stream passes through. This opening should be cut during a low-water period. Once the center opening is set, nail down an 8-inch-wide board to the two sill logs to cover the exposed wire. The completed digger dam carves, cleans, and aerates the stream pool. It will remain ice-free significantly longer than a stillwater pond.

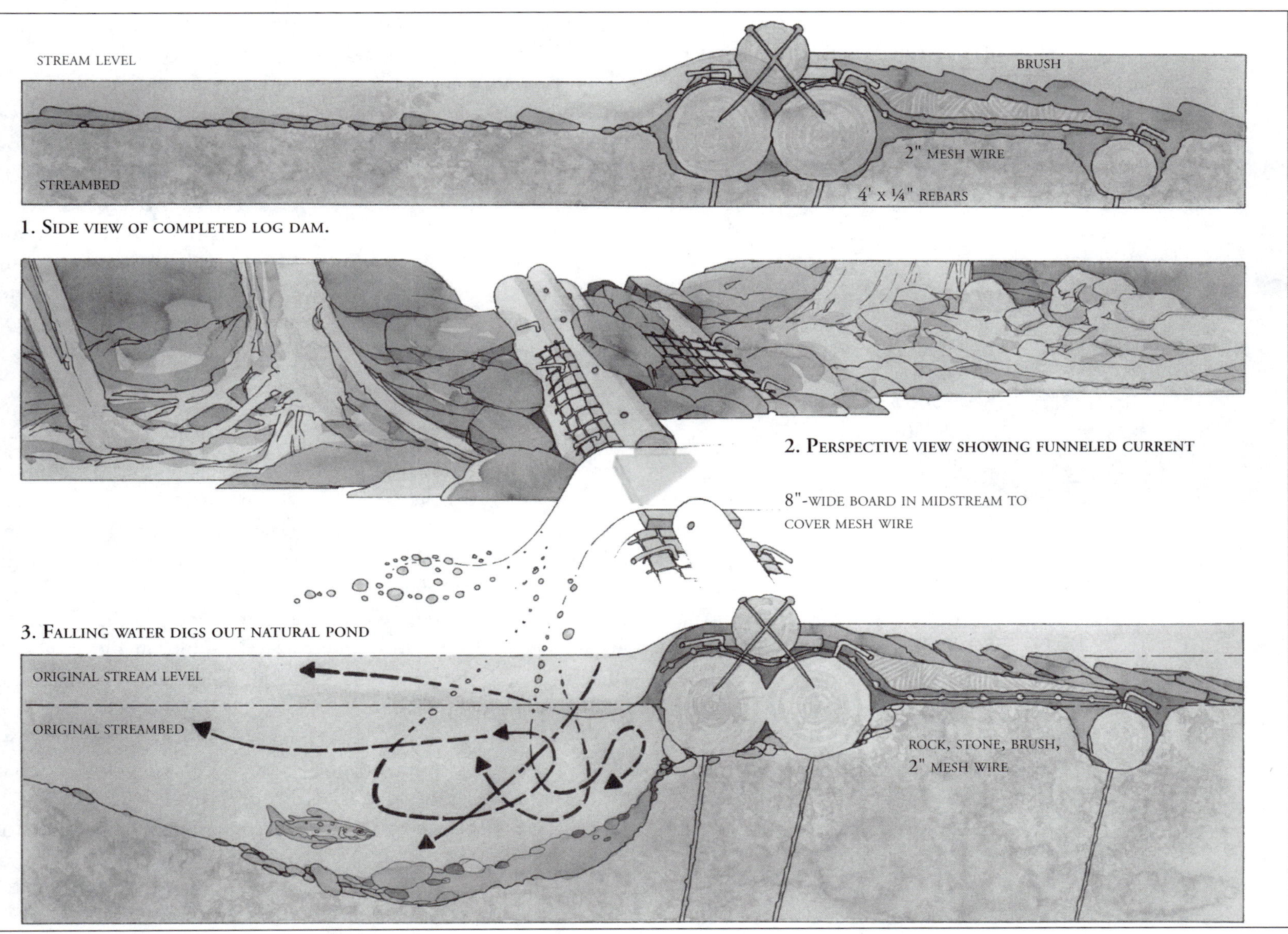

1. Side view of completed log dam.

2. Perspective view showing funneled current

3. Falling water digs out natural pond

that there are only two active sources for small-scale hydro systems in the United States and Canada (see Resources, page 111).

You need two things to make a hydro system work: head and flow. *Head* is the vertical distance between the water source and the turbine. In general, a minimum of 15 feet of head is needed to get a system operating. *Flow* is the volume of water available to the turbine, usually measured in gallons per minute. A minimum flow of 2 gallons per minute is usually required to generate usable electricity. Small-scale hydro units are frequently 12-volt DC systems, which use batteries to store electricity for use when needed. Twelve-volt lights, portable radios and TVs, and recreational-vehicle-type appliances use these systems. Larger conventional 110-volt AC household power systems require greater amounts of head and flow, and more expensive equipment as well.

EARTH PONDS VIDEO

A 200-year-old gristmill, recently converted to generate electricity. Modern compact turbines can be powered by smaller water flows.

Many successful hydro setups do not involve a pond. The water is sourced directly from a stream or brook and piped to the turbine. However, there are plenty of situations where a pond can be a good source of water for a hydro system, as long as it meets head and flow requirements. Ponds have the advantage of providing a silt- and debris-free reservoir.

To determine whether your pond or pond site has any hydro potential, you need to measure head, flow, and the pipeline distance and wire distance from the turbine to the point where electricity is needed. Head in this case is the vertical distance from the surface level of the water source to the delivery point. Head can be measured using a transit or level combined with a measuring stick. Head is usually measured in segments as you descend from water source to delivery point, then the numbers are added together. Another way to measure head is to assemble numerous garden hoses and use a water-pressure gauge to determine pounds per square inch (P.S.I.); 0.43 P.S.I. equals 1 foot of head. You can measure flow by creating a temporary dam at the pond outlet, funneling overflow into a container of known volume, and measuring the amount of time. Flow measured at different times of year will help determine generating potential during variable-flow periods. With these figures, you can then discuss system options and costs with turbine manufacturers. You should also have a rough idea of how much electricity you plan to use.

Keep in mind that 12-volt hydro systems are often used in tandem with solar cells and perhaps a backup gas generator. Hydro-solar hybrids can be effective because of the seasonal strengths of each. Hydro is usually strong in winter months, when solar is weak, and vice versa.

A few other items to consider when contemplating a hydro system: The longer the pipeline, the more expensive and difficult it is to protect, especially if freezing is a problem. The turbine may also need protection from freezing; an insulated powerhouse helps to hold heat from the water and machinery. And be careful not to draw too much water from either stream or pond, because of the adverse affect on fish and wildlife.

For the Kids: Fun and Safety

No self-respecting swimming hole should be without a swim tube or two, and I don't mean the plastic polka-dot knockoffs from Kmart. Get yourself a big black truck tire inner tube and watch your kids fight over who gets to use it first. On second thought, get two. They're durable, inexpensive, easy to repair, and they'll give your pond an aura of authentic backwoods funk, even if you live in Suburbiana. They're not bad for sliding on snow and ice, either.

Other pond gizmos that kids (and the rest of us) enjoy include belly boards, inflatable rafts, floating lounge chairs, and Styrofoam "noodles," which not only look like magnified spaghetti, but actually live up to their name, too—for our neighborhood raccoons, who seem to relish their flavor. Swim fins, snorkels, and diving masks make it fun to explore hidden treasures down among the crawfish and minnows.

Depending on the size of the pond, a canoe can be a practical craft or good training for larger bodies of water. When my younger daughter was five, she refused to go on a lake in our canoe, but when I put the canoe in the pond I couldn't keep her out of it. A pond's also a good place to practice kayaking skills, like rolling. Mini-kayaks are a perfect match for kids and small ponds. If you're lucky enough to have a tall tree close to shore, you might be able to rig up a swing. Otherwise, it's possible to build swings from poles erected over the water. Slides are also popular around ponds. Rafts, too, add a dimension to pond sports (see Floating through Summer, page 70–76.)

As long as we're on the subject of kids and water, a few words about safety. Every year our newspaper has at least one article about somebody—usually a child—drowning in a pond. The most common accident is falling through thin ice. Swimming fatalities are equally predictable, as well as boating mishaps. As a parent with two children and a pond, I've had my share of adrenaline rushes after the kids disappeared near the pond. As they've grown we've had a succession of rules about the pond. When the kids were very young, they were not allowed to go down to the water without an adult. Only after they demonstrated adequate swimming skills could they swim or canoe without a life vest. And there's still no skating or swimming alone. I'm glad our pond is within sight of the house, far enough so that it can be off-limits when necessary, close enough to be able to monitor older kids from the deck.

There's always going to be a risk factor when you mix kids and water. The best way to minimize danger is by requiring life vests for nonswimmers and making sure nobody swims, skates, or goes boating alone. It also helps if a pond has shallow edges, which reduces the risk of drowning if a youngster does tumble in. A life ring on a rope hanging on a post by the water isn't a bad idea, either. In winter, a lightweight aluminum ladder can be used to help rescue someone fallen through the ice.

You may also want to consider fencing around the pond so that kids—yours and your neighbors'—don't visit without permission. In some suburban areas, fencing may be compulsory. Check with your insurance carrier to make sure your pond doesn't qualify as an "attractive nuisance," which means that you may be liable for injuries to visitors, invited or not.

Resources

Beach building

PRODUCTS & SUPPLIERS

Geotextile Fabrics

T.C. Mirafi Group
3500 Parkway Lane, Suite 500
Norcross, GA 30092
1-800-234-0484

Synthetic Industries
4019 Industry Drive
Chattanooga, TN 37416
1-800-621-0444

Swim raft

PRODUCTS & SUPPLIERS

Floats and Hardware

Follansbee Dock Systems
PO Box 610
Follansbee, WV 26037
1-800-223-3444

International Marina Institute
35 Steamboat Road
Wickford, RI 02852
401-294-9558

Information, training, and research for the marina and boatyard industry.

Dock Hardware and Float Distributors, Inc.
PO Box 686
558 Border City Road
Geneva, NY 14456
1-800-826-3433

Dock and raft materials.

EARTH PONDS VIDEO

BOOKS & OTHER PUBLICATIONS

Docks and Projects
Edited by Ann Vanderhoof
Cottage Life Books
111 Queen Street East, Suite 408
Toronto, Ontario M5C 1S2
Canada
416-360-6880

Excellent chapter on raft and dock construction; well worth the price of the book.

Skating rinks

Snowblowers and Pumps

Echo Incorporated
400 Oakwood Road
Lake Zurich, IL 60047
1-800-432-3246

Fire protection

PRODUCTS & SUPPLIERS

Pumps

D & L Wholesale, Inc.
PO Box 1309
149 South Boulevard
Clinton, NC 28328
1-800-334-8912

General Fire-fighting Equipment

Boston Coupling
16 Bridge Street
PO Box 320
Watertown, MA 02172
1-800-538-5567

W.S. Darley & Co.
2000 Anson Drive
Melrose Park, IL 60160-1087
1-800-323-0244

KENYON CONSTRUCTION CO.

Irrigation

PRODUCTS & SUPPLIERS

Pumps

Aquacenter, Inc.
166 Seven Oaks Road
Leland, MS 38756
1-800-748-8921

Aquatic Eco-Systems, Inc.
1767 Benbow Court
Apopka, FL 32703
1-800-422-3939

AG Engineers, Inc.
29 Alnut Crest Road
Gorham, ME 04038-2640
207-854-2481

D & L Wholesale, Inc.
PO Box 1309
149 South Boulevard
Clinton, NC 28328
1-800-334-8912

DripWorks
231 East San Francisco Street
Willits, CA 95490
1-800-522-3747

Drip irrigation systems and comprehensive catalog.

Echo Incorporated
400 Oakwood Road
Lake Zurich, IL 60047
1-800-432-3246

Irrigro
1555 Third Avenue
Niagara Falls, NY 14304
905-688-4090

Drip irrigation systems, surface and subsurface. Also supplies aeration equipment.

The Ram Company
HCR 61, Box 16
Lowesville, VA 22951
1-800-227-8511

Extensive selection of hydraulic rams, including do-it-yourself kits. Also offers solar water pumps for moving water naturally in flat country, and drip irrigation tubing.

Shindaiwa, Inc.
PO Box 1090
Tualatin, OR 97062
503-692-3070

Agricultural irrigation pumps including PTO pumps for tractors.

Wade Rain
PO Box 23666
Portland, OR 97281
1-800-222-7246

BOOKS & OTHER PUBLICATIONS

Cottage Water Systems
by Max Burns
Cottage Life Books
111 Queen Street East, Suite 408
Toronto, Ontario M5C 1S2
Canada
416-360-6880

Excellent primer on all aspects of developing a household water system, including a good section on pumps.

The Home Water Supply: How to Find, Filter, Store, and Conserve It
by Stu Campbell
Storey Communications
Schoolhouse Road
Pownal, VT 05261
1-800-441-5700

A fine guide to water-system development, including a well-illustrated section on pumps.

Watering Systems for Lawn & Garden
by R. Dodge Wilson
Storey Communications
Schoohouse Road
Pownal, VT 05261
1-800-441-5700

Thorough coverage of mechanical and gravity irrigation systems; overhead and drip. Lacks a source guide.

Raising fish

SUPPLIERS

The following fish suppliers represent a small sample of the many hatcheries and fish farms across the United States. Depending on the species and age, fish may or may not be able to be shipped long distances or across state lines. In my experience, the closer the hatchery, the better the chance for success. It is important to be aware that stocking nonnative species has the potential to endanger local fish, if the fish enter the larger population. A supplier who has seen your pond firsthand is going to have a pretty good idea of its potential. Be sure to discuss with hatchery personnel the best species, size, disease resistance, and stocking rate for your site. For a more comprehensive listing of fish suppliers, check the annual Buyer's Guide of *Aquaculture* magazine (see page 108). Your state extension service may also be able to make recommendations.

Common Carp

Northeastern Biologists
1 Vern Road
Rhinebeck, NY 12572
914-876-3983

Owen & Williams Fish Farm, Inc.
Route 1 Box 249
Hawkinsville, GA 31036
912-892-3144

Stoller Fisheries
Box B
Spirit Lake, IA 51360
712-336-1750

Valley Fish Farm
PO Box 601
Brawley, CA 92227
619-344-5049

Grass Carp and White Amur

Farm Cat, Inc.
PO Box 317
Lonoke, AR 72086
1-800-530-7931

Florida Fish Farms, Inc.
9684 CR 705
Center Hill, FL 33514
904-793-4224

Keo Fish Farms, Inc.
PO Box 123
Highway 165N
Keo, AR 82083
501-842-2872

J.M. Malone & Son Enterprises
PO Box 158
Lonoke, AR 72086-0158
501-676-2800

Owen & Williams Fish Farm, Inc.
Route 1 Box 249
Hawkinsville, GA 31036
912-892-3144

Channel Catfish

Austin Farms
PO Box 1590
306 Main Street
Indianola, MS 38751
601-887-5398

Ken's Fish Hatchery
Route 1
Alapaha, GA 31622
912-532-6135

Malone's Catfish Fingerling Co.
PO Box 287
Highway 31 South
Lonoke, AR 72086
501-676-2800

Opel's Fish Hatchery
PO Box 51
Worden, IL 62097
618-459-3287

Bullhead Catfish

Opel's Fish Hatchery
PO Box 51
Worden, IL 62097
618-459-3287

Silver Creek Aquaculture
2526 CR 262 North
Henderson, TX 75652
903-889-3406

Largemouth Bass

Aquatic Control, Inc.
PO Box 100
Seymour, IN 47274
812-497-2410

Danbury Fish Farms
PO Box 528
Danbury, TX 77534
1-800-460-8414

Farm Cat, Inc.
PO Box 317
Lonoke, AR 72086
1-800-530-7931

Hickling's Fish Farm
RD Box 201-A1
Edmeston, NY 13335
607-965-8488

Ken's Fish Hatchery
Route 1
Alapaha, GA 31622
912-532-6135

Laggis' Fish Farm, Inc.
08988 35th Street
Gobles, MI 49055
616-628-2056

Bluegills

North Star Fish Hatchery
Montour, IA 50173
515-492-6159

Southland Fishers Corp.
600 Old Bluff Road
Hopkins, SC 29061
803-776-4923

Micanopy Fisheries
Route 1, Box 591
Micanopy, FL 32667
352-591-1650

Danbury Fish Farms
PO Box 528
Danbury, TX 77534
1-800-460-8414

Brook Trout

Alléghany's
2755 Grand Lignes
St. Philemon
Quebec G0R 4A0
Canada
418-469-2823

Fernwood-Limne, Inc.
77 Saratoga Road
Ganswoort, NY 12831-1034
1-800-233-1282

Hinchin Brooke Fish Hatchery
RFD 1 Box 1010
Chatauguay, NY 12920
518-497-6505

Paradise Brook Trout Co.
RD 1
Cresco, PA 18326
717-629-0422

Rainbow Trout

Beitey Enterprises
3502 Beitey Road
Valley, WA 99181-9740
509-935-6100

Big Brown Fish Hatchery
PO Box 584
Route 115
Effort, PA 18330
610-681-6660

Castaline Trout Farms
Route 1 Box 151
Goshen, VA 24439
703-997-5461

Crystal Lake Fisheries
Route 2
Ava, MO 65608
417-683-2301

Hy-on-a-Hill Trout Farm, Inc.
PO Box 308
Plainfield, NH 03781
603-675-6267

Lost River Trout Farm
5787 West 5000 North
Mackay, ID 83251
208-588-2866

Warlick Trout Farm
East Bethel Road
Randolph, VT 05060
802-728-5065

EQUIPMENT & GENERAL INFORMATION

Aquatic Eco-Systems, Inc.
1767 Benbow Court
Apopka, FL 32703
1-800-422-3939

Manufactures the backyard Fish Farm recirculating system.

Bird-X
300 North Elizabeth Street
Chicago, IL 60607
1-800-662-5021

Bird and pest control.

Hach Company
PO Box 389
Loveland, CO 80539
1-800-227-4224

Test kits for water analysis.

Plow and Hearth
PO Box 5000
Madison, VA 22727-1500
1-800-627-1712

Reed-Joseph International
Box 894
Greenville, MS 38702
1-800-647-5554

Bird & pest control

Stoney Creek Equipment Co.
11073 Peach Avenue
Grant, MI 49327
1-800-448-3873

General equipment for aquaculture.

Trout Unlimited
1500 Wilson Blvd., Suite 310
Arlington, VA 22209
703-522-0200

Offers guidance to pond owners regarding trout stocking, with an emphasis on using local fish populations and avoiding nonnative species.

BOOKS & OTHER PUBLICATIONS

American Currents
North American Native Fishes Association
123 West Mount Airy Avenue
Philadelphia, PA 19119
215-247-0384

Dedicated to furthering knowledge of native American fishes.

Aquaculture: The Farming and Husbandry of Freshwater and Marine Organisms
by Bardach, Ryther, and McLarney
John Wiley & Sons, Inc.
605 Third Avenue
New York, NY 10158

Premier textbook on aquaculture.

Aquaculture Magazine
16 Church Street
Asheville, NC 28801
704-254-7334

Stories target commercial aquaculture, but an indispensable reference for fish hatcheries. Get the annual Buyer's Guide.

Backyard Fish Farming
by Bryant, Jauncy, Atack
Prism Press
2 South Street
Bridport, Dorset DTG 3NQ
England

Catfish Ponds and Lily Pads
by Louise Riotte
Storey Communications
Schoolhouse Road
Pownal, VT 05261
1-800-441-5700

Farm Pond Harvest Magazine
1390 North 14500 E Road
Momence, IL 60954
815-472-2686

Excellent source of information about raising fish, and ads for fish hatcheries.

Fish Farming News
PO Box 37
Stonington, ME 04681
207-367-2490

"The business newspaper for North American aquaculturists" is commercially oriented, and an interesting source of articles and ads.

General Principles of Aquaculture
by Huner, et al.
Food Products Press / Haworth Press
10 Alice Street
Binghampton, NY 13904
1-800-342-9678

Good aquacultural reference book from a press with other related titles.

Home Aquaculture: A Guide to Backyard Fish Farming
by Steven D. Van Gorder and Douglas J. Strange
Alternative Aquaculture Association, Inc.
PO Box 109
Breinigsville, PA 18031
610-395-8202

How to grow backyard fish without a pond, using recirculating tanks. Also publishes the Alternative Aquaculture Network Newsletter.

McClane's Field Guide to Freshwater Fishes
by A.J. McClane
Henry Holt & Co., Inc.
115 West 18th Street
New York, NY 10011
Excellent reference to inland fishes with vivid color illustrations.

Ray Troll's Shocking Fish Tales
Illustrated by Ray Troll
Text by Brad Matsen
Ten Speed Press
PO Box 7123
Berkeley, CA 94707
1-800-841-2605
If you love fish and fishing, this bizarre and fascinating book of piscine history, anecdote, and art is sure to please.

Small Ponds in Connecticut: A Guide to Fish Management
by Brian Murphy and Donald Mysling
Connecticut Department of Environmental Protection
Maps and Publications Office
79 Elm Street
Hartford, CT 06106-5127
203-566-7719

Aquaculture Information Center
National Agriculture Library
USDA, Room 304
1030 Baltimore Boulevard
Beltsville, MD 20705-2351
301-504-5558
Monographs, books, and information.

International Center for Aquaculture
Publications Office
203 Swingle Hall
Auburn University, AL 36849-5419
205-844-4786
Excellent source of aquacultural books and information.

Pondscapes

PRODUCTS & SUPPLIERS

Outdoor Furnishings

Adirondack Wood Furnishings
PO Box 608
Malone, NY 12953
1-800-280-1541

Frontgate
2800 Henkle Drive
Lebanon, OH 45036-8894
1-800-626-6488
Catalog supplier of upscale waterside furniture, including a floating pool recliner for those who find inner tubes too declassé.

Gardener's Supply Company
128 Intervale Road
Burlington, VT 05401-2850
1-800-955-3570

Plow & Hearth
PO Box 5000
Madison, VA 22727
1-800-627-1712

Preferred Living
Clermont County Airport
Batavia, OH 45103-9747
1-800-543-8633
Outdoor furniture and water toys.

Smith & Hawken
PO Box 6900
Two Arbor Lane
Florence, KY 41022-6900
1-800-776-3336

Bridges and Gazebos

BowBends
PO Box 900HS
Bolton, MA 01740
508-779-2271

Dalton Pavilions, Inc.
20 Commerce Drive
Telford, PA 18969
215-721-1492

Vixen Hill Gazebos
Main Street
Elverson, PA 19520
1-800-423-2760

Architectural and garden ornaments.

Christine Sibley
15 Waddell Street NE
Atlanta, GA 30307
404-688-3329

Kenneth Lynch & Sons
84 Danbury Road
PO Box 488
Wilton, CT 06897-0488
203-762-8363

Fountains

Aquacenter, Inc.
166 Seven Oaks Road
Leland, MS 38756
1-800-748-8921

Aqua Art
PO Box 14167
2020 Manchester Street
Atlanta, GA 20234
404-873-2822

Stoney Creek Equipment Co.
11073 Peach Avenue
Grant, MI 49327
1-800-448-3873

Otterbine Barebo
3840 Main Road East
Emmaus, PA 18049
1-800-247-8837

Hot Tubs and Saunas

Snorkel Store Company
4216 Sixth Avenue South
PO Box 20068
Seattle, WA 98102
1-800-962-6208

Snorkel's cedar and redwood tubs combined with a woodstove are ideal for outdoor use.

BOOKS & OTHER PUBLICATIONS

Garden Design Magazine
100 Avenue of the Americas
New York, NY 10013
1-800-234-5118

Gazebos
Creative Homeowner Press
24 Park Way
Upper Saddle River, NJ 07458
1-800-631-7795

Gazebos and Other Outdoor Structures
Creative Homeowner Press
24 Park Way
Upper Saddle River, NJ 07458
1-800-631-7995

Gazebos and Other Garden Structure Designs
Sterling Publishing Co., Inc.
387 Park Avenue South
New York, NY 10016
1-800-367-9692

Sheds: The Do It Yourself Guide for the Backyard Builder
by David Stiles
Camden House / Firefly Books
PO Box 1338
Buffalo, NY 14205
1-800-387-5085

The Sauna
by Rob Roy
Chelsea Green Publishing Co.
PO Box 428
White River Junction, VT 05001
1-800-639-4099

Simple Garden Projects
by Terence Conran
Crescent Books
Random House Value Publishing
40 Engelhard Avenue
Avenel, NJ 07001
1-800-726-0600

Traditional Garden Woodworking
by Peter Hollard
Sterling Publishing Co., Inc.
387 Park Avenue South
New York, NY 10016
1-800-367-9692

Hydropower

PRODUCTS & SUPPLIERS

Energy Systems and Design
PO Box 1557
Sussex, New Brunswick E0E 1P0
Canada
506-433-3151

Harris Hydroelectric Systems
632 Swanton Road
Davenport, CA 95017
408-425-7652

Fun and safety

PRODUCTS & SUPPLIERS

Water safety devices and small craft suited for ponds.

Cabelas
812 13th Avenue
Sidney, NE 69160
1-800-237-4444

L.L. Bean
Freeport, ME 04033
1-800-221-4221

The Boundary Waters Catalog
105 North Central Avenue
Ely, MN 55731
1-800-223-6565

Excellent source of canoes, kayaks, life vests, and other stillwater equipment. One of my favorite catalogs.

KENYON CONSTRUCTION CO.

4. WILDLIFE

Build a pond, step back, and wildlife happens. Whether you like it or not. Most people build ponds knowing that some increase in wildlife activity will come with the transformed territory. It could mean deer coming to the shore for a drink, geese or ducks laying over during migration, peepers singing on a spring night. But you may not be so eager to welcome beavers or muskrats, which can do significant damage. And there are those folks who envisage their pond as a swimming pool, and want nothing to do with being nibbled by a minnow or feeling mud between their toes.

However, unless you cover your pond with a plastic bubble, some kind of animal immigration is inevitable. Frogs will come, and salamanders, and most likely one day you'll find minnows darting around the water, deposited perhaps by a bird who ate fish eggs elsewhere and then used your pond as a rest stop.

If you'd prefer to keep the pond relatively wildlife-free, don't incorporate design elements that attract them. The less aquatic vegetation, the less the food to sustain and attract wildlife. The same goes for shoreland grasses, brush, and trees. Don't build a pond in a wetland or remote wooded area, and don't stock fish, which also attract critters.

On the other hand, wildlife that does come is often invisible. Last year a moose took a two-hour bath in our pond. Alas, we were on vacation and didn't know until we got home and heard about it from our neighbors, who had watched from a nearby field. My kids said they wished we'd been home to see it, and I agreed, although I explained that the moose probably came precisely *because* we were away. Our lifetime list of visitors we have seen includes various ducks and geese, kingfishers, herons,

EARTH PONDS VIDEO

Blue heron arriving for dinner

Opposite: *With a good inflow and sufficient size, a pond can serve the many masters of fishing, swimming, boating, and wildlife attraction. As a general rule, a good pond is worth three times its construction cost in raising your property value. Note the small basin (left) where silt settles out of the inlet water.*

osprey, deer, turtles, an endless supply of frogs, and a few leeches. When I'm stocking trout I try to discourage the herons and kingfishers by using scare-away balloons, with a little backup from the dog. I once had an unexplained loss of trout during the winter. It could have been an otter or muskrat, or perhaps a raccoon, but there's no way of knowing for sure what happened under the ice. Another invisible visitor. The leeches did a disappearing act, too, gobbled up no doubt by a combination of fish, frogs, and crawfish.

What follows is a collection of resources for pond owners who want to manage wildlife. It's divided between attracting critters and keeping them away. Every pond will have its own particular mix, depending on the aims of the owner, the persistence of the wildlife, and the vagaries of the seasons.

Wildlife Pond Design

Ponds designed for wildlife can be as small as a backyard frog pond or as expansive as a created wetland teeming with fish, turtles, beavers, and waterfowl. No matter what size, however, a successful wildlife pond will include the two basics of wildlife survival: food and cover. That means having the right kind of edge, where a majority of the food will grow, and plants, shrubs, and trees to supply cover. Creating a successful edge environment usually means making sure the submerged soil is fertile to encourage plant growth and establishing a shallow water depth.

Wildlife ponds are often allowed to seed themselves, particularly if sited in a marshy area where wetland plants like cattails and aquatic grasses already grow. The new pond will then be colonized by neighboring plants. But some ponds may need a jump start, especially if the owner is in a hurry to attract wildlife. Wetland nurseries and water-garden suppliers offer a variety of plants attractive to wildlife as well as to the eye.

A small frog pond should not include fish, which eat up the eggs. However, if you intend to attract birds such as herons and kingfishers, stock your pond with minnows and crawfish, and perhaps bigger fish. Ponds designed to attract waterfowl should be larger, with an ample food supply. Wildlife ponds should be secluded, away from human activity as well as domestic animals. The cleaner the water, the better.

In *Landscaping for Wildlife,* Carrol Henderson suggests including a shallow area featuring brush piles and rocks for amphibians, as well as a stretch of mowed grass for sunning waterfowl. In my own pond I've noticed that a float or, even better, a dock offers frogs a pleasant hangout, as well as shelter and shade for fish. It's also important to make sure you provide a shallow, gravelly area for the waterfowl, which require grit for digestion.

Naturally enough, a forested pond will attract woodland animals such as deer, fox, and raccoons. Beavers, otters, and muskrats may also show up. More-open pond sites invite waterfowl.

Permitting may be necessary, but the fact that it's a pond designed for wildlife should work in your favor.

Adapting an existing pond to wildlife uses may not require any permitting, except in the case of significant terrain or stream alteration.

Planting for Wildlife

Anybody who has set out bee balm in a flower garden and then watched the hummingbirds zero in knows the value of plant power in attracting wildlife. If you apply the same strategy to a pond, you can attract waterfowl and other wildlife with equally dramatic results. Instead of bee balm, however, you'll be using aquatic vegetation, moist-soil plants, and shrubs that provide food and cover.

Deciding which plants to introduce to your pond habitat involves first determining the capabilities of the pond, primarily climate and soil quality. If you live in the North you won't have much luck with tropical water lilies; conversely, you won't be able to

FRANK FRETZ

grow cranberries in the South. Soil fertility and texture are also important considerations. There's little chance of growing moist-soil plants in gravel or sand, no matter how wet the terrain, and soil that has been heavily compacted during pond construction will also give disappointing results.

Bear in mind that some plants can take over a pond, covering the surface with a tangle of vegetation that might delight the ducks but will horrify anglers and swimmers. For example, several types of pondweed, as well as some native lilies, make excellent wildlife food but often get out of control. Small ponds are most likely to be overrun; periodic maintenance is essential to curtail invasive plants.

In addition to selected aquatic plantings, plants, shrubs, and trees can be used to create buffer strips around a pond. Buffer strips help stabilize banks and reduce erosion; they slow runoff, take up nutrients, and filter soil particles that might otherwise contribute to sedimentation or nourish nuisance vegetation. Buffers can provide shade and food for fish, as well as wildlife habitat, including food, nesting, and cover. They can also enhance privacy.

The first thing to do before creating a planting scheme is to be sure *not* to cut down potentially useful native trees or shrubs already present. In the process of building a new pond, especially, think twice before you cut. The tree you down for a better view this spring might turn out to be worth keeping for shade this summer or wildlife cover next winter. Native species also have the advantage of having already proved themselves hardy (unless newly elevated water levels do them in). Keep in mind, too, that a wooded shoreland generally benefits wildlife, but the trade-off may be more leaves and branches in the water. Many pond owners resist the lyrical willow tree because of the substantial debris it sheds.

Trees and Shrubs

Trees that do well in the kind of moist soil that surrounds a pond include red maple, red osier dogwood, tamarack, cedar, larch, poplar, cottonwood, alder, willow, and several species of oak. The oaks are an important source of nuts, and dogwood produces fall fruits.

Valuable moist-soil shrubs include elderberry, cranberry, chokecherry, winterberry, and spicebush, all of which produce fruits enticing to wildlife, including game and songbirds. And don't forget that only a few yards from the pond you may find well-drained soil suited to other trees and plants valuable to wildlife, such as beech, black cherry, sumacs, and blueberry.

Aquatics

The animals and birds you want to attract to your pond require two essentials: food and cover. If you're interested in attracting ducks, sago pondweed is perhaps the top food plant. Its early-season seeds and late-season tubers provide food for dabbling and diving ducks, as well as for swans and geese. Fish also benefit from this popular pond plant, finding shelter and shade in its vegetation and nourishment from insect larvae deposited on the stems. Arrowhead, or wapato duck potato, is another excellent all-around wild duck food. An emergent plant with attractive arrow-shaped leaves and white flowers, it produces seeds, shoots, and tubers beneficial to geese, swans, and diving and dabbling ducks. Muskrats also feed on the tubers and like to build their houses near arrowhead beds. Several Native American tribes depended on the arrowhead's starchy tubers, harvesting and drying them in the fall for cooking in the winter months. They can be boiled, roasted, or baked. The plant is also valuable as a bio-filter, absorbing nutrients and pollutants.

When I asked Pat Kester, of Kester's Wild Game Food Nurseries, to recommend the top wildlife plants, in addition to arrowhead and sago pondweed, she suggested bulrush and bur reed, two tall plants notable for nesting cover. Bulrush provides both food and cover for ducks (as well as blinds for hunters). It supplies food and house-building materials for muskrats and cover for game fish. Its vigorous root system and thick stems also make an effective erosion antidote, breaking wave action and encouraging other aquatic growth. The bulrush is reputed to act as a valuable bio-filter, and is a component of many natural wastewater-treatment lagoons.

The cornlike seeds of bur reed are eaten by waterfowl and marsh birds, and muskrats use the entire plant for food and building material. Insect larvae and other small aquatic organisms live on their underwater stems. It also provides blinds for hunters. Like the bulrush, which is actually a sedge and not a rush, the name *bur reed* is misleading because the plant does not have a burr that sticks to your clothing and your dogs.

Cattails and Others

Although it doesn't provide edible seed for waterfowl or marsh birds, the cattail offers just about everything else a wetland critter might need. Its rhizomes are a highly desirable muskrat food, while its foliage is used for their houses. Its flowers, which look more like cigars than cat tails, provide a cottonlike fluff that marsh birds use for nesting material. Red-winged blackbirds like to attach their nests to the stout stalks. They provide excellent cover for waterfowl and upland game birds, and blinds for hunters. They offer a bounty of food for humans as well. The rhizomes can be cooked or processed into a flour reputedly containing more protein than corn and rice and more fat and minerals than corn, rice, and wheat. The rhizomes produce shoots that can be eaten like asparagus, and the flowers and pollen are also edible. You can even gather your cattails in a basket made of cattail leaves, and then sit back after dinner on a chair with a cattail cane seat!

Several other pond plants deserve mention. Among the submergents (plants that live under water), consider coontail (hornwort), elodea, and muskgrass. These are excellent sources of feed for waterfowl, and they provide oxygen, cover, and a food-growth medium for fish. Emergent plants (foilage above water) include wild celery, watercress, smartweed, duckweed, and pickerelweed. Beware: These aquatics can be extremely invasive. The smaller and shallower your

Planting Guide

	PLANTS	ATTRACTS	OTHER USES	POSSIBLE PROBLEMS
AQUATICS	Arrowhead (wapato, duck potato)	ducks, geese, swans, muskrats, beavers	bio-filter	may be invasive
	Bulrush	ducks, geese, swans, muskrats	bio-filter; cover for fish and birds	may be invasive
	Bur reed	ducks, geese, pheasants, muskrats, deer, beavers	shoreline stabilization; cover for fish and birds	may be invasive
	Cattails	geese, muskrats, beavers	cover for waterfowl, marsh birds, fish; spawning for fish; soil stabilizer; hunting blinds	may be invasive
	Coontail	ducks, geese, swans, marsh birds, muskrats	cover for fish	may be invasive
	Duckweed	ducks, geese, pheasants, beavers, muskrats, small mammals		may be invasive
	Elodea	beavers, waterfowl	oxygenates water; fish cover; harbors insects for fish	may be invasive
	Pickerelweed	waterfowl, muskrats	cover for fish	may be invasive
	Sago pondweed	ducks, geese, swans, shorebirds, muskrats, beavers, moose	cover for fish, amphibians, reptiles	may be invasive
	Smartweed	ducks, geese, marsh birds, aquatic shorebirds, fur bearers, small mammals, wild turkeys	erosion control	may be invasive
	Watercress	waterfowl, beavers, muskrats, deer	harbors organisms that trout feed on; cover for small fish	may be invasive
	Water lily	ducks, muskrats, beavers, porcupines, moose, deer	food and cover for game fish; harbors insects	may be invasive
	Wild celery	ducks, swans, muskrats	food and cover for fish and aquatic invertebrates	may be invasive

	PLANTS	ATTRACTS	OTHER USES	POSSIBLE PROBLEMS
SHRUBS AND TREES	Alder	birds, waterfowl, beavers	nitrogen fixing	
	Blueberry	songbirds, bears, game birds, foxes, mice, skunks, deer, chipmunks	human food	
	Cedar	deer, birds, mammals, mice, butterflies	offers cover for many animals and birds	
	Chokecherry	songbirds, mammals, game birds		
	Cottonwood	birds, waterfowl, mammals	tree cavities for wood ducks	
	Cranberry	songbirds, mammals, game birds	cover	
	Elderberry	songbirds, game birds, mammals	human food	
	Oak	birds, mammals, waterfowl	food, cover, nesting; tree cavities for wood ducks	
	Red maple	birds, waterbirds, squirrels, chipmunks, mammals	tree cavities for wood duck	
	Redosier Dogwood	birds, game birds, deer, mammals	streambank stabilization	
	Spicebush	songbirds, game birds, deer		
	Willow	birds, mammals, game birds, waterfowl	streambank stabilization; tree cavities for wood ducks	leaf litter
	Winterberry	songbirds, mammals, game birds, deer	cover	
MOIST-SOIL PLANTS	Cardinal flower	hummingbirds, orioles, butterflies		
	Joe-pye weed	butterflies, bees		
	Sweet flag	waterfowl, muskrat	soil stabilizer	
GRAINS	Millet	waterfowl, upland game birds		requires annual planting
	Wild rice	waterfowl, birds, muskrat		does not do well in land-locked ponds; requires annual planting

pond, the quicker it can be taken over by aquatic plants. You will have to decide how much of your pond, if not all of it, you want to dedicate to wildlife plants. And then you may have to wait for the plants to agree or disagree. Plants that can be introduced to the shore include switchgrass and various sedges for cover and millet for food.

There's more to pond plants than simply generating wildlife food. Aquatic and moist-soil plants can be enjoyed for their appearance (see Garden Ponds, page 151). Many of the food and cover plants mentioned in this chapter are attractive in their own right. Witness the extensive use of cattails and various rushes, reeds, and sedges by landscape architects and water gardeners. Furthermore, some highly decorative plants do double duty as wildlife attractors. Water lilies are a popular water garden plant, and several hardy varieties produce seeds favored by ducks, as well as tubers enjoyed by muskrats. Game fish find cover under their floating leaves; insect life thrives among submerged stems. Again, be aware that water lilies can be invasive.

Joe-pye weed is a tall plant that thrives in moist soil, at pond edges, and in slowly moving streams. Its large, faded pink flowers rival milkweeds when it comes to attracting butterflies. The cardinal flower, a tall plant with bright red later-summer flowers found in rich moist soil, is a hummingbird magnet. Sweet flag is an aromatic plant with foliage similar to that of cattail and iris, and small, mustard yellow flowers. Favoring shallow water and pond edges, it provides cover for waterfowl and food for muskrats. Its spicy-sweet citrus scent once made it valuable as a strewing herb, cast on the floor of pioneer cabins to freshen the air. It was also used as a medicinal plant, flavoring for candies, and scent for candles. Vivid blue flowers on a 1- to 2-foot spike distinguish pickerelweed, a hardy native aquatic that thrives at the edges of shallow ponds, in streams, and in marshes. Wild ducks like its seed, as did Native Americans, who used it for cereal and flour. It is also valued as a cover for game fish, among them—as the name implies—pickerel. Deer feed on the stalks. On the other hand, pickerelweed is reputed to be highly invasive, and harbors mosquito larvae as well.

A few closing thoughts. The best wildlife attractors in the world may be nullified at a pond pestered by dogs and cats. If you're a neophyte at wildlife planting, nursery catalogs are great for colorful descriptions and photos, but a few good books will provide a reality check about the difficulties and downsides of various plants. And don't forget to check out your local nurseries. Many plant experts advise buying species from within a 100-mile radius or so of your site, to enhance adaptation.

Attracting Waterfowl

If you're hoping to use your pond to attract waterfowl, think big. Waterfowl need ponds to help supply food, nesting areas, and protective cover. Ponds covering much less than an acre aren't likely to attract waterfowl for lengthy stays. That's not to say that smaller ponds won't serve as stopovers for migrating birds, or perhaps as a brief pairing location; you may find that a small secluded woods pond with plenty of wetland vegetation will attract nesting waterfowl. However, bigger is better when it comes to supporting waterfowl over time. Fortunately, that doesn't necessarily mean laying out vast sums of money for large ponds. Ponds designed for waterfowl don't need to be as deep as conventional impoundments, so it's possible to save money on excavation and still come up with the required surface size.

Whether you're interested in attracting geese, wood ducks, mallards, or other waterfowl, all birds use ponds to fulfill several basic functions. They choose them for pairing up, nesting, rearing young, and—depending on your location—wintering over. Most birds will use different ponds for many of these requirements, going from one to another as the reproductive cycle evolves. A pond that is good for pairing may not offer the cover needed for nesting, and yet another pond may be best for rearing the young. Northern ponds are good locations for mating and raising young; southern ones, for wintering over.

In general, a pond attractive to waterfowl will be generous in size, with ample shallow areas providing both submergent and emergent vegetation and native food. It will be sufficiently protected from human disturbances and predatory pets.

In addition to providing an attractive pond, landowners can enhance sites with artificial nesting structures. Agriculture, lumbering, and development have eliminated many natural nesting areas in woodlands, fields, and shore areas. Waterfowl respond well to constructed nesting platforms.

This wood-duck box has been built to correct specifications and includes a necessary predator shield, but it may not be as attractive to a nesting hen as one installed over water. If it doesn't attract a wood duck, it may still provide a home for other waterfowl or land birds.

Wood Ducks, Divers, and Dabblers

Perhaps more than any other waterfowl, wood ducks take to managed ponds and nesting structures. Hunted to the brink of extinction in the last century, they've been nursed back in large part due to conservation programs and hunting limits. Now found in most areas of the United States, except the arid West and Rocky Mountains, their population is thriving.

CONDO FOR DUCKS

This sophisticated wood duck box, designed by Mr. Don "The Duckman" Helmeke, provides extra ventilation for setting hens. Kits may be ordered from Don at 15702–105th Avenue N, Maple Grove, MN, 55369. Simpler designs are offered by the U.S. Fish and Wildlife Service and Ducks Unlimited (see p. 141).

Lumber:

1. Use "grade 3" cedar, rough one side.
2. Sides/front/back/ floor: 1" x 10" (actual ¾" x 9¼").
3. Roof: 1" x 12" x 13" (actual ¾" x 11¼" x 13").
4. Rough surface faces out on completed house.

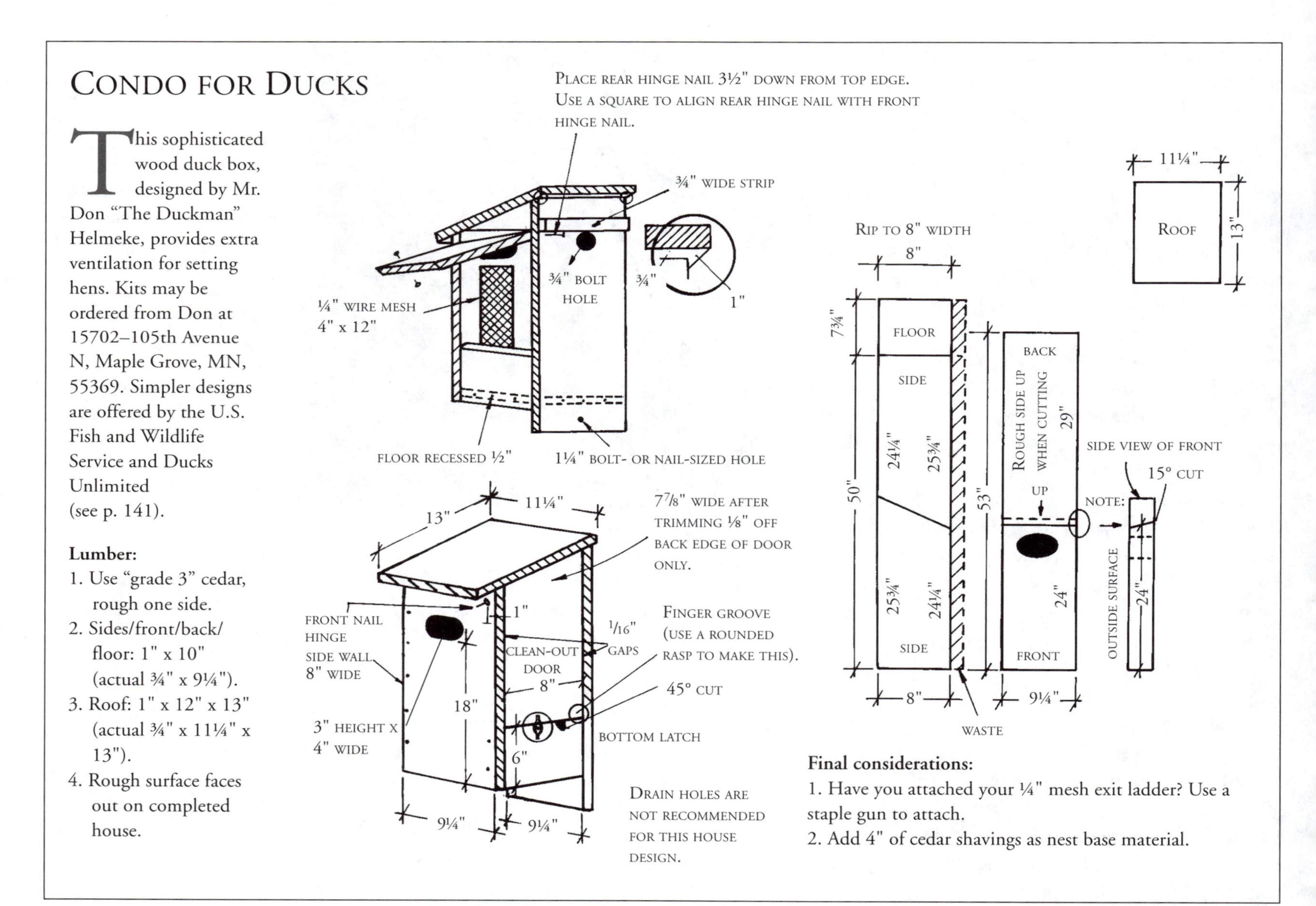

Final considerations:

1. Have you attached your ¼" mesh exit ladder? Use a staple gun to attach.
2. Add 4" of cedar shavings as nest base material.

MINNESOTA DEPARTMENT OF NATURAL RESOURCES

Wood ducks, also known as woodies, naturally nest in tree cavities near water. Basswood, soft maple, cottonwood, some oaks, and black willow are among their favorites. However, many of these natural nesting areas have been lost to development, hence the popularity of the wood-duck box. A relatively simple wooden box mounted on a post or tree satisfies the nesting requirements of wood duck hens. The box is usually constructed of a rot-resistant wood such as cedar or redwood, or treated lumber. Using 1- by 12-inch material, a conventional box is 12 inches wide by 24 inches tall and 10 inches deep, with the roof slanting down slightly toward the front. Inside, just below the 3½- to 5-inch hole, a strip of hardware cloth is installed so that the newborn ducklings can follow their mother out. The hole is about 19 inches above the floor. If the box is mounted on a pole, using steel or plastic will help give the slip to climbing predators; a wood pole requires a predator guard below the box. Predator guards are usually inverted metal cones fitted around the support pole to keep animals from reaching the box. A 3-foot wrapping of metal flashing below the box should also work. Trees or poles can be in the water, usually near shore, or set back as much as ½ mile from water, as long as there are no obstacles to prevent ducklings from getting to water. Boxes should be mounted at least 3 feet above the high-water line; some experts recommend as much as 20 feet on living trees. Eschew aspens, poplars, and alders, as they're likely to be toppled by beavers. Early March is the best time for both mounting and cleaning the boxes. Boxes should be placed far enough from each other to be out of sight, to discourage egg "dumping" by upset hens. Hens will occasionally lay their eggs in other hens' boxes and then abandon them if they feel overcrowded. This overwhelms the resident hen's ability to incubate her eggs.

Ponds and boxes don't guarantee wood duck immigration. One spring morning I accompanied a couple of wildlife biologists doing maintenance on a series of wood-duck boxes around a secluded Vermont pond. They hauled an aluminum ladder through mud and puckerbrush, past beaver lodges and over feeder streams, stopping at each tree where the boxes had been mounted. They climbed up and cleaned out the nests and checked the remaining eggshells to determine nesting species. What they found was everything but wood duck eggs: starling nests, blue jay feathers, and hooded merganser eggs. It was a good lesson in evolution. Wood ducks face tough competition from other nesting birds, and once they do set up housekeeping they've got predatory raccoons and blue jays to watch for.

In addition to providing a well-made box, and a predator guard if necessary, be sure to line the nest with bedding material. Straw or hay—with the exception of alfalfa, which rots easily—makes a good liner, as does a mix of wood chips and sawdust. It's important to clean out and refill each nest with fresh material every spring before the ducks arrive. Install the boxes at a ratio of about one per acre to start with, although more can be added, and be sure to keep them away from overhanging branches, which can provide access for attacking predators.

There's no guarantee when and if wood ducks will occupy your boxes, and fish and wildlife biologists reminded me that other waterfowl species should be considered welcome as well. It may take several years for woodies to find your newly erected structures, and 50 percent residency is considered good. Once the birds establish themselves, hens and juveniles often return year after year to the same refuge.

In addition to woodies, which are considered perching ducks, there are diving ducks (canvasback, lesser and greater scaup, ring-necked duck, bufflehead, redhead, goldeneye, and ruddy duck) and dabbling ducks (mallard, black duck, gadwall, green-winged and blue-winged teals, northern pintail, American wigeon, and northern shoveler). You can attract both divers and dabblers to your pond. Diving ducks tend to prefer deeper impoundments, while dabbling ducks feed in marshier sites, flooded agricultural fields, forested wetlands, and rivers. Both like a combination of grains, plants, and aquatic invertebrates such as snails and clams.

However, unlike woodies, dabbling and diving ducks prefer to nest in natural areas such as cattail clumps, on top of muskrat houses, and in upland grasses. These birds will also be attracted to islands in ponds or wetlands. Permanent islands can be built using earth or rocks, or by using artificial materials such as culvert pipe, upended and filled with soil, and round hay bales. Floating islands are also built with lumber or logs, or vegetation, and then anchored in place. Islands afford a large degree of protection from predators, which is important for ducks that cannot defend their nests. Seed islands with grasses to provide nesting material, or provide it in other ways.

Mallards and other ducks are also attracted to artificial baskets and cylinders. These structures are usually mounted on poles or posts, again with predator guards if necessary. The nests must be lined with bedding material and cleaned every spring. (Annual maintenance is necessary to nesting success.)

In the Midwest and South, where waterfowl overwinter, landowners interested in attracting waterfowl often manage flooded fields and wetlands. Croplands can be seeded with grains like millet and rice and flooded to produce food for waterfowl. As in the North, nesting structures can be built to attract birds.

Geese

Like ducks, geese are inclined to winter over where grain croplands are adjacent to forested wetlands, ponds, and grassy weedy areas with a diversity of water depths and native food. In these areas fields and croplands can be managed to produce large and small grains, similar to those favored by ducks. The less the geese are disturbed by human activity, the more they will be attracted to an area.

To attract geese to nesting sites, earthen islands are highly favored, especially those that are sheltered from prevailing winds and placed far enough off-

WATERFOWL NESTING RAFT

Floating structures provide loafing sites for geese and goslings and have the advantage of not being affected by water level fluctuation. But they may be susceptible to ice damage if not removed each fall, may be moved or damaged by storms, and are vulnerable to muskrat damage. Note the 6- by 4-inch slot cut in the side to allow goslings to exit the nest; without this escape hatch, the goslings will not survive. A dozen or so holes should be punched in the bottom of the tub for drainage, and it should be filled one-third with sawdust and topped with a cushion of grass or wild hay just before nesting season. Do not use the washtub for a turtle and duck loafing platform.

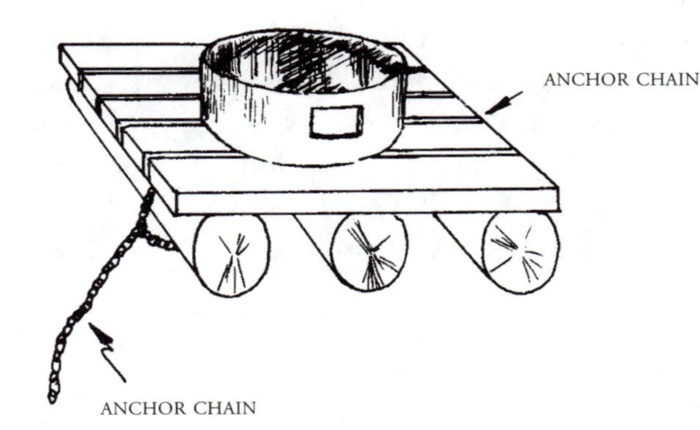

Materials:
One 8"-diameter cedar pole, 12' long
Four 2" x 6" x 8' boards
One 22"-diameter round metal washtub

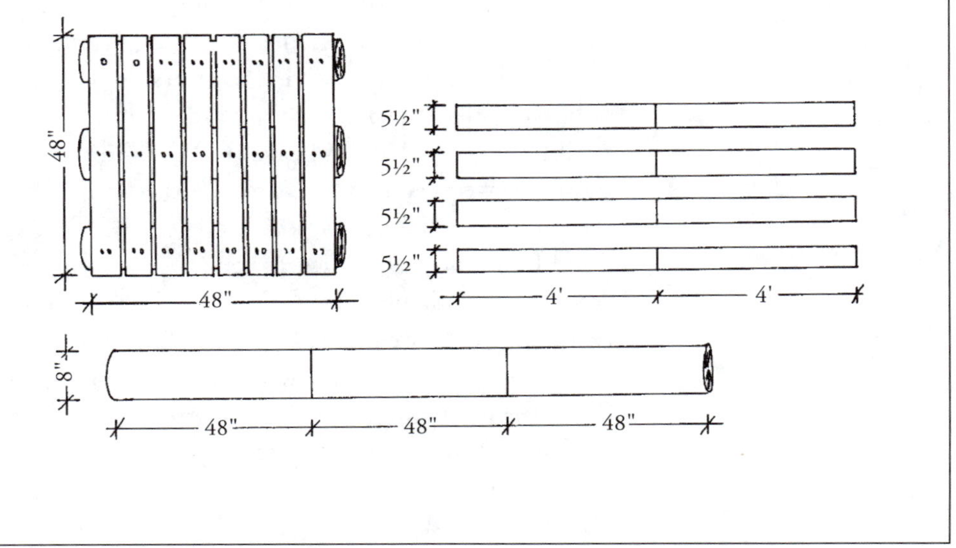

MINNESOTA DEPARTMENT OF NATURAL RESOURCES

shore to afford protection against predators. Like ducks, geese will also use less expensive "islands" of round hay bales tipped on end, or soil-filled culvert pipe. Post-mounted structures are economical to construct but not as durable. Since geese nest earlier than mallards and other ducks, they may occupy spaces intended for ducks unless the nests are divided into separate compartments. Nest materials include straw, hay (not alfalfa), and a mixture of bark and wood chips. Geese will also use muskrat houses for nesting.

Beaver Management

There's so much irony involved in the beaver–pond keeper relationship that it's hard to know where to begin. The early settlement of North America was supported, in large part, on wealth extracted from beavers: directly, from the riches generated by the sale of beaver pelts and glandular oil; indirectly, due to the fertility of arable land in beaver meadows. Because of trapping, we very nearly extirpated the animal from the continent. To add insult to injury, we borrowed its pond-building techniques to build our own reservoirs. The fundamentals of good pond design, essentially copied from beavers, include building a dam that allows enough overflow to prevent flooding and the creation of supplementary silt catchment and recharge pools upstream. But let a beaver decide to take up residence in one of "our" ponds, and watch out. We've learned their building methods, but we're only beginning to figure out how to coexist peacefully.

Considering the benefits of beaver engineering, it's not surprising that landowners would like to get along. If you're setting aside a pond exclusively for wildlife, you may be happy to include beavers in the mix. Beaver ponds are home to a variety of wildlife, and the wetlands they create and inhabit enhance the environment through water storage and flood abatement. In fact, a healthier beaver population might have prevented the midwestern floods of 1993. According to hydrologists Donald Hey and Nancy Phillipi, "If only a third of the 40 million beavers that once occupied the Upper Mississippi Valley survived today, the disastrous floods of 1993 would not have occurred." They calculated that beavers in the 456-million-acre valley maintained 51 million acres of ponds in 1600 and "at a depth of 3 feet, the original ponded area could have stored more than three floods the size of the 1993 event . . . [T]he current beaver population may pond only about ½ million acres."

A less theoretical example of helpful beaver engineering was recently cited in *The Beaver Defenders Newsletter,* a publication of the Unexpected Wildlife Refuge, Inc. (see Resources, page 144):

> In Cucumber Gulch, near Breckenridge, in 1986 the Breckenridge Ski Area, then owned by Aspen Ski Corp., started construction of a Superchair ski lift. Within a year, what had been a near-pristine, beaver-pond-dominated

ecosystem was fast turning into a wasteland. The water turned brown, gravel-laden runoff filled all but two of about 12 beaver ponds, making it impossible for the beavers to live. Wildlife and fisheries habitat was destroyed and water quality severely degraded. Some natural erosion occurs in any valley, but the beavers deal with it [by] making their dams higher.

When one man downstream sued Aspen Ski Corp. because of poor water quality, they were about to build a $2.5 million retaining pond to catch runoff. Instead, they solved the problem by restoring beavers to Cucumber Gulch. Seven beavers were reintroduced, and they began work immediately. There are now an estimated 30 beavers in the gulch, and after five years the restoration process has turned out to be such an overwhelming success that it is considered a model project by Colorado wildlife officials.

But it's one thing to admire them in a neighboring wetland and quite another to find them in your own pond. Mother Nature has put millions of years into designing these dam builders, and they're not only obsessed with blocking flowages, but they're also stubborn.

When a beaver moves into a man-made pond, all hell—including the dam—can break loose. Led by instinct to raise water levels to create ponds deep enough for security and food storage, beavers may plug overflow pipes and earthen spillways, making the water levels higher than you intended. Add a heavy rainstorm or snowmelt and you have the formula for flooding, which may lead to damage downstream, the destruction of the pond, or both.

Beaver damage is not limited to pond structure. Those neatly chewed trees you see lying on the shore supply dam-building material as well as food, and a colony of beavers will go through all appetizing trees within 100 yards of your pond before moving on to another location. Aspen, alder, poplar, and willow are a few of their favorites. To make matters worse, the beavers often take their time about felling timber, girdling a tree here and there, taking the weekend off, and

The appearance of a beaver dam in or near your pond may be a welcome sight or a horror, depending on your plans. If your ambition is to create a wildlife pond, beavers may be welcome; if it's a recreational pond, beavers can cause trouble by plugging overflow and inflow channels and chewing up your scenery.

The Clemson beaver pond leveler is one of the most successful beaver control devices. It adds a protected cage to the intake pipe puncturing a beaver dam. This makes it possible to drain a beaver pond completely, or set a level that both man and beaver can live with, without resorting to lethal eradication.

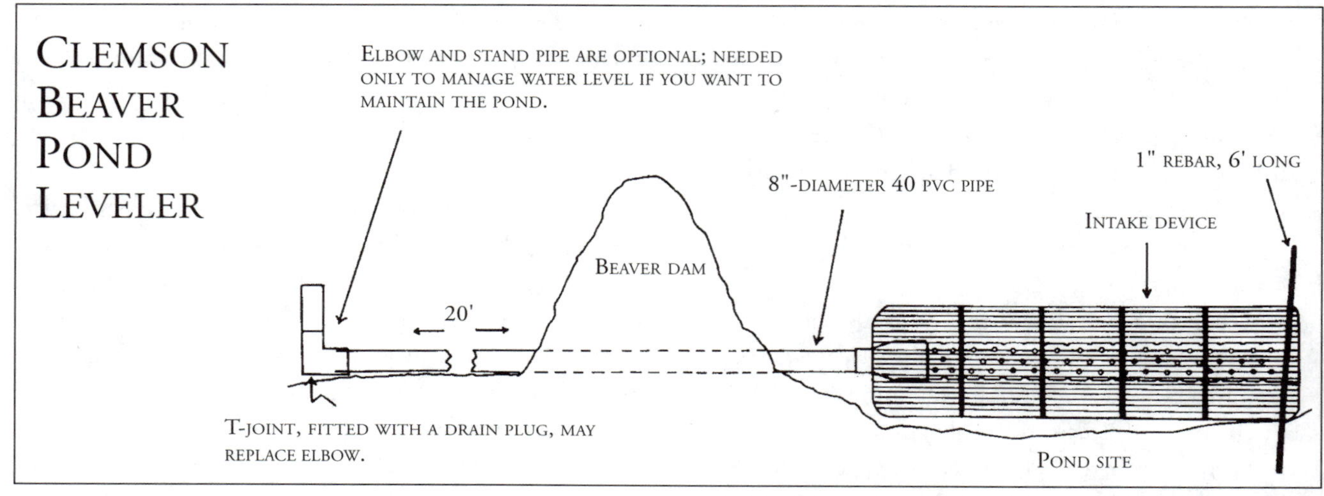

GENE W. WOOD, DEPT. OF AGRICULTURE, FISHERIES, AND WILDLIFE, CLEMSON UNIVERSITY

reporting again Monday morning. One pond owner who had spent all summer reconstructing his spillway system in an attempt to coexist with a beaver colony told me he'd been hiking around his pond on a windy Sunday afternoon when a half-chewed poplar came loose and slammed down an arm's length away. It might be time to start cutting off their food supply, I suggested. This can be done by removing all desirable trees within 50 to 100 yards of the pond, or by wrapping the trees with heavy-duty mesh fencing to a height of 4 feet. To be most effective, the cylindrical fencing should stand out from the tree a foot or so, with props to maintain the beaverproof space. (The height is necessary to prevent beavers from standing on snow or debris to reach the trunk.)

In addition to damaging the pond basin and peripheral vegetation, beavers can contaminate the water itself. Beavers are often held responsible for spreading giardiasis, a waterborne intestinal disease that humans can pick up from drinking water or when swimming. Some scientists report, however, that giardiasis may have as much to do with human fecal contamination as beaver waste. Tularemia is another illness beavers carry, although it is transmitted only through direct contact.

Not long ago a neighboring farmer shot a beaver damming up a stream running through the middle of his hayfield. The beaver had built up an impressive dam, and my children and I had enjoyed watching him at work while we waited for the morning school bus. Needless to say, I had a hard time explaining the shooting, although I did my best to justify it on account of the farmer's worries about losing his field. Imagine my dismay when, the very next spring, he clear-cut the alder along the stream and chipped it up for mulch. Had he cut the alder first, the beaver would have left on his own.

It's true that most farmers have a knee-jerk reaction when it comes to getting rid of beavers. The old-timers have hands-on experience when it comes to the negative economics of flooded fields and roads, and they rarely hesitate to employ the "high-speed lead" solution, or worse. Everything from used motor oil to dynamite has been employed to eradicate beavers. However, a few farmers are attempting to get along—with some surprising results. A New Hampshire vegetable grower recently allowed a beaver colony to maintain a lodge and pond near one of his cornfields. During the drought of 1995, while other growers lost their crops, his corn thrived on groundwater impounded by the beavers.

Despite potential problems, many landowners go out of their way to accommodate beavers. In some cases, the motive is altruistic; for others it's a question of complying with the law. Some states allow landowners to shoot or trap beavers; others forbid even live trapping and removal because it often transfers the problem to someone else. Consider also the issue of "ownership." Beavers don't care much about property lines, as Phyllis A. Bellmore points out in her booklet, *Baffling Beavers: Solutions to Beaver Flooding Problems.*

> When a person purchases a piece of property, control is taken of this piece of land without much thought of the natural link that binds the property to another person's property. It may be that this piece of property has a beaver's lodge and dam, and the owner fears flooding problems. He wants the beavers destroyed. This property could be an extension of an adjoining wetland area—a natural link binding the two properties. The adjoining property owner would like to solve the problem so that the beavers might remain. Who will protect the beavers? What agency will speak for them? What is right and wrong, wise and foolish, fair and unfair?

Be sure to check with your state fish and wildlife department—and your neighbors—before beginning any beaver-removal regime, not only for legal clearance, but also to benefit from state and federal animal management programs and literature.

Damage Control

Your overflow system will determine how you can prevent damaging damming. If your pond flows out over an earthen spillway, that's usually where beavers will build a dam. Manual removal of the dam often degenerates into a frustrating contest of wills—by day you tear it apart, by night they repair it. If the dam they've built impounds a large watershed, you may need permission from your state Natural Resources

Department to take it down, particularly if the concurrent release of water could have an adverse effect on downstream habitations, roads, or fish.

Instead of getting into an endless tug-of-war, a better approach might be to breach the beaver dam with a "beaver pipe." A beaver pipe is any kind of device driven into the dam to cause it to leak. It may be a cluster of parallel logs; a long wooden box with wire mesh underneath; or, perhaps most efficiently, perforated plastic pipe. These materials have proved effective at thwarting the beavers' ability to repair leaks. Perforated pipe appears to be the material of choice these days when attempting to accommodate beavers and yet establish a safe level of water somewhat below their desired threshold. Depending on the size of the blockage, one or more pipes are inserted through the dam, or the dam is taken apart to the desired water level and the pipe installed. You can install several pipes in tandem, with submerged elbows at the upstream end to further discourage plugging. A pair of steel fence posts and a crosspiece support the intake. The beavers will usually reconstruct the dam, and the pipe will set a new water level despite their efforts. Beaver pipes work best in watersheds of 10 acres or smaller, where heavy rainfalls will not exceed the pipe discharge capacity. And they may not work in shallow earthen spillways where the beavers can bury them in mud. Shallow spillways may benefit more from being deepened, thus lowering your pond water level and that of subsequent beaver dams. Cordoning off a spillway channel, or culvert, with wire mesh fencing is another tactic, although it may require periodic cleaning. I've also heard that electric fencing works.

Piped overflows present a different challenge. If they're located in deep water, a steel grille guard over a vertical drain may be enough to deter beaver blockage. However, a culvert or drain close to shore may be easier for the animals to bury in sticks and mud. Protecting these outlets may require a beaver baffle. One of the most effective baffle designs is the Clemson pond leveler, a protected pipe that is coupled to the overflow. The device combines perforated pipe and a wrapping of heavy-duty hog fencing, which is installed upstream of the dam. Clemson baffles are often used to drain beaver ponds completely. In man-made ponds, a vertical elbow on the downstream end of the pipe will sustain a desired water level. Most trash guards and baffles require some maintenance. Depending on the severity of the problem, this could mean cleaning off debris periodically, weekly, or even daily.

Another drainage system getting good reviews is the Control Structure™. Available from Agri Drain Corporation, this overflow system is intended for embankment ponds where a vertical box can be installed in the berm. Water exits the pond through a pipe installed 5 feet or more below the pond water level. From there it rises up and over an adjustable gate inside the control structure box and then siphons out the exit pipe. This system outsmarts beavers because the outlet is underwater, where they don't normally plug pipes; and it doesn't make any noise to trigger the beaver's dam-building instinct. It also exhausts cold, low-oxygen, high-silt water, which creates a better environment for fish and cuts down on alga nourishment.

Installing a beaverproof overflow doesn't guarantee the end of your problems. Beavers may decide to build additional ponds above and/or below the pond you just repaired, which can again threaten water quality and overflow systems. Or they may decide they like your pond, despite the baffles, and build a lodge next to your diving board. This is about the stage when old-timers go for the rifle. But before you start shooting (with permission, if required), consider a few last-ditch alternatives. Your fish and wildlife department may be able to locate someone who can live-trap the animals for relocation, or you might try it yourself using Tomahawk traps. Chemical repellents have also shown some promise when applied to resident beaver scent mounds. (Beaver mounds are territorial markers somewhat the equivalent of an off-limits sign. The wrong smell on a beaver mound may persuade the resident to leave.) Another technique is sterilization, either by surgery or by hormone implant. However, this requires live-trapping, a trip to the vet, and funds that you may not want to spend. Some beaver advocates are now encouraging fish and wildlife departments to fund a sterilization program. One desperate woman I know first tried live-trapping and then shooting. The beavers still came back. Finally, guilt-stricken, she began hanging wind chimes all around her pond. She heard somewhere that beavers can't stand the racket. For her sake, I hope there's a steady breeze in the backyard.

If you feel you must resort to lethal trapping, the Conibear trap is recommended by some wildlife experts. In their Animal and Plant Health Inspection Service (APHIS) booklet *Beavers,* James E. Miller and Greg K. Yarrow suggest the Conibear No. 330. "Not all trappers will agree that this type of trap is the most effective; however, it is the type most commonly used by professional trappers and others who are principally trapping beavers. This trap kills beavers almost instantly . . . Appropriate care must be exercised when setting and placing the trap. Care should also be taken when using the Conibear type traps in urban and rural areas where pets (especially dogs) roam free. Use trap sets where the trap is placed completely underwater."

Defensive Siting

If all this is beginning to sound like a warning against pond building, you're right. At least not on the wrong site. Over the past few years we've been hearing about the irreplaceable value of wetlands, and if you haven't heard, take a look at your state's environmental laws. After decades of being drained or filled to accommodate developers and highways, most remaining wetlands are off-limits. It's a good thing, too. Wetlands support wildlife, mitigate flooding, and cleanse and reserve water. However, wetland protection laws were not usually written with pond builders in mind, and most agencies recognize the ecological value of creating a pond. It's often possible to go through the permitting processes and come out the other side with a permit to build a pond, as long as the wetland is not deemed irreplaceable. In fact, transforming a small wet sag into a pond is usually a plus for the environment.

However, when I'm asked to design a pond for a wetland area, I put up a caution flag. With a beaver on it. Unless you intentionally want to attract them—and understand the potential negative effects—why ask for trouble? If the site offers the kind of vegetation beavers favor, or if the site borders known beaver territory, beware. Across the country there's a beaver population explosion. Beavers are building dams on New England interstates, chewing down landscape nurseries in Indiana, and generally doing a good job of making up for all those generations lost to hunting and trapping. Lack of predators, low pelt value due to antifur sentiment, and more people moving to the country all add up to a rising potential for conflicts between beavers and humans.

Muskrats

There's a song called "Muskrat Love," but you're not likely to hear it from anyone who's been invaded by a tribe of those cattail-chomping rodents. Muskrats are a largely forgotten creature, except by a few trappers and anyone who finds his pond water a shade muddier than usual, and perhaps a bit leaky as well.

Muskrats are mostly herbivorous, and they love pond plants. They'll gobble your carefully waterscaped garden pool or pond and even dig burrows in the basin, which may cause leaks. In some cases they eat fish.

Muskrat control ranges from eliminating protective shoreline brush, grass cover, and edible vegetation to trapping. Removing cattails is a highly recommended passive-resistance technique. So is installing a layer of riprap or galvanized wire mesh along the shoreline to a depth of 3 feet below the surface and a foot above. Electric fencing is another option.

Muskrats often come along with beavers, and many of their control techniques are similar. (Otters and raccoons can also prey on fish, and may require similar removal strategies.) Your fish and wildlife department and APHIS office should be able to offer suggestions and information, as will conservation outfits such as Beavers, Wetlands & Wildlife (see Resources, page 144).

Attracting Amphibians

What's a pond without a chorus of peepers greeting the arrival of spring, or a couple of big old bullfrogs croaking back and forth across the water on a hot August afternoon? And if you've got kids, you'll appreciate how well a few frogs lazing in the shallows can keep them entertained.

Frogs seem to find their way naturally to most ponds, along with turtles and toads. The toads are especially welcomed by gardeners, who know how effectively they gobble up cutworms and slugs. Because of their complex life cycles and need for live food, amphibians respond less to an offering of feed or plants than to protection from predators, such as game fish, which eat their eggs. I've also owned a number of cats and a dog who occasionally appeared at the door with a half-eaten frog carcass. Herons and other waterfowl, too, can put a dent in the frog population.

Establishing safe basking sites for amphibians may be the most effective way to attract and secure them. Partly submerged offshore snags and brush piles make predator-proof islands. A sunny north shore of a pond is a good place to set rocks in and out of the water, drawing frogs to their protective warmth.

From larva to tadpole to full-blown amphibian, frogs undergo such a dodgy development that it's a challenge even for professional growers to raise them. They need different food at varying stages, and it's got to be alive. Flies, minnows, and crawfish are all appreciated. The pH must not be too acid (6.5–6.9). A

Swamp, bog, marsh, or fen: They're all wetlands, providing habitat for wildlife, storing floodwater, and improving water quality. After 200 years of dredging, filling, and draining, half the original wetlands in the U.S. have disappeared. However, recently public awareness of wetland values has undergone a dramatic turnaround. State and federal laws protect our remaining wetlands, and new wetlands are being created for wildlife habitat and water quality improvement.

recent decline in the frog population has led some to blame acid rain. It's possible to sweeten acid ponds with agricultural limestone and organic matter, but other possible causes of the frog decline are tougher to remedy on a local level. Heightened UV radiation caused by ozone depletion is one, as well as the obvious carnage caused by automobiles, especially during spring breeding when frogs are migrating.

On the other hand, who says you can't make a difference, even if it's just with a small backyard "frog pond"? Stock it with native aquatics such as cattail, arrowhead, water lily, marsh marigold, and duckweed. Then watch the frogs and toads proliferate—and the cutworms and slugs disappear from your garden.

Wetlands

I ran into a contractor the other day at the village store. We'd worked on several ponds together, and I hadn't seen him in a while. It was early morning, he was filling up his pickup, and he was in a hurry. I asked him how things were going and he shrugged his shoulders. "I've got a few ponds lined up," he said. "I want to get them finished." He got in and started the truck. "Before we can't build them anymore." He quickly drove off. I didn't have to ask him what he meant. In my work with pond builders over the past few years, commiserating about the difficulties of getting permits has become topic number one. Building a pond that doesn't leak used to be the main subject. Now it's wetland regulations and their impact on pond construction.

During the past decade or so, the federal Clean Water Act and state laws across much of the country have been enacted to discourage tampering with wetlands. These laws are meant to be a corrective to hundreds of years of wetland filling, draining, and dredging, which have effectively cut in half the original wetland acreage in the United States. Ironically, in an effort to prevent shopping malls from displacing what's left of our wetlands, regulators are also preventing some people from building ponds. True, ponds aren't exactly wetlands. But they're not Wal-Marts, either.

What makes wetlands so special? In recent years scientists and landowners have become aware that wetlands play a vital role in the ecological health of the planet. Yes, they're a breeding area for mosquitoes and leeches and get in the way of agricultural and municipal development. But what you lose by eliminating them is worse. Wetlands act like giant sponges, soaking up rainfall and runoff, thereby retarding flooding. They recharge aquifers and release water during drought. They stabilize shorelines, filter out pollutants, and cleanse the water. They provide refuge for wildlife and enhance biodiversity. If rain forests are Earth's lungs, wetlands are her kidneys.

Laws protecting wetlands vary, but the regulation process begins with designation. Many wetlands are mapped and given a value designation, either by federal or state agencies. The more pristine and ecologically significant, the more off-limits. Permits to alter protected wetlands may be granted, depending on the nature of the area and the construction project. It's been my experience that ponds often receive a green light, once the permitting process runs its course.

In the case of federally protected wetlands, according to Section 404 of the Clean Water Act, the goal is "no net loss." When wetland construction is permitted, mitigation is often required. In other words, tit for tat. Subtract a wetland here, and you're obliged to add an equal one, usually nearby. These situations often involve large construction projects, and have led to a new industry of wetland construction.

The idea of "building" a wetland strikes some people as arrogant. Mother Nature makes wetlands; how can we possibly come up with something as complex? But until we decide to halt development, it seems like a moral obligation to try. Besides, if beavers—the original wetland creators—can do it with their bare paws and sharp teeth, we just might have a chance, too.

Perhaps the most interesting aspect of this new building industry is the development of practical applications for wetlands. Artificial marshes are now used around the world as low-cost natural systems for cleaning municipal waste, as well as to improve the quality of drinking water. Originally pioneered in Germany in the early 1970s, man-made marshes are designed to simulate natural wetlands in which aquatic plants are known to absorb pollutants and purify the water. A wetland can be designed to receive municipal sewage, wastewater from food-processing industries, partially treated drinking water, or polluted river water. Suspended solids settle to the bottom of these wetlands and microbiological reactions occur, cleansing the water of nutrients, nitrogen, and phorphorus. The "polished" water can then be released back into the watershed or channeled into reservoirs. Designing these systems is still an experimental science, and unlike chemical treatment plants, each one must be tailored for a unique situation. Recent successful systems include a multipond wetland designed to clean up water from the Trinity River in Texas, where it's then used to augment municipal drinking water. An artificial peat wetland in northern Minnesota is cleaning up water polluted by heavy metals and ethylene glycol. In Tampa, Florida, wetlands drained for agricultural use are being restored to help purify drinking water. At a construction cost ranging from 50 to 90 percent less than chemical treatment plants, and with significantly lower operating costs, the lure of these wetland systems is obvious.

Considering these attributes, why aren't we seeing wetlands replace sewage plants everywhere? The difficulties include size. More acreage is required for a wetland treatment system than a chemical plant. In cold weather, the biological purifying processes slow down, making them more problematic in northern climates. And some substances, including ammonia and heavy metals, are difficult to remove. Equally significant, many state regulatory agencies simply haven't acquired the expertise to supervise these installations. There are also lingering questions about the possible negative effects on wildlife in these waste-treatment wetlands.

Might we be simply putting a fancy label on the same old bad habit, namely slinging garbage into the nearest swamp?

Flood prevention is an unquestioned wetland attribute. Researchers working on the Des Plaines River in Illinois found that a 5.7-acre marsh can handle the annual runoff from a 410-acre watershed, leading them to suggest that wetlands might solve flood problems better than the more expensive levees and dikes now in use. They calculated that if only 3 percent of the Mississippi River watershed had been restored to wetland, the flood of 1993 would not have occurred. In addition to being cheaper to construct than dikes and levees, wetlands offer the bonus of providing habitat for wildlife, including a diverse environment in which many species of endangered plants and animals thrive. Constructed wetlands also offer opportunities for recreation and educational use.

So what's all this got to do with ponds? Considering that some of the best pond sites are in wetlands, a lot. A pond site may be a small, temporarily wet hollow or sag, or a pristine peat bog rimmed with rare orchids. You may find yourself planning to build a pond on a site that requires a state or federal permit, or it might be simply wet enough to require a permit, leaving you to make a judgment call about seeking permission. I don't have a problem digging a pond in a soggy swale that doesn't support much in the way of wildlife or plants. A pond there has a better chance of increasing the overall biodiversity. On the other hand, it seems reasonable that the bog should be left intact. Meanwhile, I've heard enough horror stories about pond builders digging out a marsh without permission, getting caught, and paying a fortune for wetland restoration to recommend going through the legal hoops.

Still, you have to wonder about the owner of the bog. How is he supposed to feel about paying taxes on a piece of property he can't use? Depends on the owner. Some people would be happy to play host to a marsh teeming with wildlife. Others might agree with the spirit of the law, but question their property tax bill. Thus have wetlands become a lightning rod for political extremists. Conservative politicians use them as scapegoats for overreaching government, and environmentalists hail them as sacred cows. Efforts at compromise include states where use-value tax abatement gives protected wetland owners a financial break. "Wetland banks" are also being used by builders obliged to mitigate construction projects: Developer X joins other developers buying into a large wetland restoration. Wetland banking may be more ecologically efficient and financially sound than is trying to create from scratch a relatively smaller wetland equal to the one disturbed.

As for that pond you want to build in a wetland: It all hangs on the classification of the wetland and what kind of pond you want to build. If a permit is required, you may want to discuss incorporating some wetland features into the pond to ensure that the new body of water will equal or improve lost wetland features. If your pond site turns out to be in a highly protected wetland, spend some time learning about what a valuable resource you possess. It just might make it easier to let it be.

Wetland Permits

If your pond site lies in a wetland, one or more permits may be required to alter the area. The best procedure is to follow the food chain up, beginning with your local town government. Check with the town clerk to see what permits may be required, and then inquire at the state level. One of the best sources of information will be your state Water Resources Board. The Environmental Department may also be able to help. From there you may find yourself referred to the local USDA NRCS office, where federal wetland inventory maps should reveal the status (if any) of your site. Depending on the classification of your pond site, you may have to deal with the US Army Corps of Engineers, which regulates wetland construction for the Environmental Protection Agency.

The Pond According to Rusz

You're thinking you'd like to design a pond to attract wildlife, or perhaps to retrofit an existing pond. You don't mind the thought of supplying an oasis for whatever needy critter happens along, be it a colorful wood duck or mallard, or a scruffy muskrat intent on digging holes in your dam and ravaging the cattails. In fact, you wouldn't mind dedicating the entire pond to wildlife if necessary.

Zoning your pond into shallow and deep areas creates habitat for wildlife as well as swimmers.

So what to do? You could follow the conventional wisdom of landscape designers and nursery salesmen, namely to import an expensive array of aquatic grasses and plants in the hope of magnetizing your quarry. Or you might buck the tide and heed Patrick Rusz's alternative approach. Rusz is chief biologist with the Michigan Wildlife Habitat Foundation. He's been working with many of the state's private landowners who are interested in improving wetland habitats for wildlife, especially waterfowl. His philanthropically funded organization has been taking up the slack where government environmental programs have cut back. However, Rusz's approach differs radically from the traditional emphasis on attracting waterfowl and wildlife through extensive aquatic and moist-soil plantings. "Forget plantings," says Rusz. "Concentrate on pond design."

According to Rusz, the ideal wildlife pond should have a large area that's 18 inches deep or less. You could take that as a cue to design the entire pond as a shallows, although Rusz points out that landowners surveyed about pond design are generally not content with shallows-only ponds. In fact, where water levels drop significantly in summer, designing a shallows-only pond that won't go dry in August may be the biggest challenge of this approach.

A two-tiered design—shallow and deep—seems to work best. Since most ponds are not perfectly circular, rather than creating a shallow shoreline ring, you'll come up with one end dedicated to wildlife and the other for fish and folks. In the North, where ponds can freeze 2 to 3 feet down, 10 to 15 feet is considered a healthy depth for the deep end. The shallow end will freeze solid, but that won't affect waterfowl who've gone south.

The transition from shallow to deep should not be gradual, says Rusz, again contradicting traditional pond-design principles. "Gradual slopes are fertile grounds for undesirable weeds," he points out, "and in fact the slope acts like a slide, carrying nutrients from the rich wildlife areas where they're needed to the fish potholes, where they're not." In other words, a quarry-like hole is preferable. To keep organic matter from slumping out of the shallows, Rusz suggests installing a "speed bump." Imagine an underwater berm between the shallows and the deep area, a barrier perhaps 6 inches or so below water level, dividing the 18-inch wildlife area from the remainder of the pond.

Size is also important in wildlife ponds. If you want to combine deep water for fish and a shallows for wildlife, anything much less than an acre overall is likely to be unsatisfactory. Rusz's own 2-acre pond combines three zones of differing depths: a shallow area for wildlife at one end; the deepest fish habitat in the center; and a rather flat wading and swimming area, including a beach, at the other end. He emphasized that his fish hole is steep sided.

For people who already own a pond, following Rusz's advice may mean restructuring the basin. If the pond includes a suitable water control structure, this could involve something as simple as a permanent drawdown to create a shallow area. But for others it will involve modifying the shape. It may be possible to shortcut the construction process, digging in water with a dragline or hydraulic excavator, but it's a slow and messy approach that may not yield the clean structural contours Rusz recommends. Work in the dry for best results.

Critters don't live on water alone. The pond must include plant life, and plants need fertile soil in order to grow. If soil fertility isn't a problem, most of the plants will come on their own. After all, that's how Mother Nature handled things before people started imitating beavers. But if your pond is too sandy or stony, it's possible to beef up the fertility. Rusz suggests that ditch scrapings make a pretty decent soil amendment, and you can't beat the price, especially if your town road crew is looking for a convenient disposal area. Try to select scrapings that haven't been contaminated by road salt. Clay is another good source of nutrients, and noted for engendering cattails, so beneficial to good waterfowl activity. Rusz is skeptical about the need for extensive transplanting, but he does stress the need for a good cattail fringe for food and cover. Hay and straw also improve pondbed fertility. Of course, too many nutrients could be as bad as too few. Moderation is a virtue in pond management.

In the North, the traditional delivery method for nutritional "detritus" is via the ice drop. When the ice is thick enough to support a pickup or tractor, layer the clay, soil, or hay over the area to be fertilized and let the spring sun do the delivery. In England, waterfowl enthusiasts are having success unrolling straw and hay bales on the ice. When the grass settles, it creates a fertile emulsion that is beneficial to wildlife.

Rusz mentions only two plants worth intentionally adding to the pond fringe: cattails and, farther upland, switchgrass. The rest, including the highly touted sago pondweed, he feels would happen on their own or they won't be missed. However, he does suggest installing nesting cavities for ducks: boxes for wood ducks and open-ended cylinders for mallard hens (see Attracting Waterfowl, page 120–26).

Finally, a word about fish. "Good wildlife habitat equals poor fish habitat," Rusz warns. Shallow depths are not conducive to fish, he explains, especially in the North. In fact, some fish can exacerbate alga problems. Bluegills, for instance, feed on the zooplankton that otherwise would graze on phytoplankton, more commonly recognized as scummy summer algae. If you must have fish, trout and bass make better partners for that new population of immigrant wildlife.

Resources

Wildlife pond design

Seed, Rootstock, and Plants

J & J Transplant Aquatic Nursery
PO Box 227
Wild Rose, WI 54984-0227
414-622-3552

Submergent and emergent plants, including some hard-to-find species like jack-in-the-pulpit and wild leek. Specializes in propagating, harvesting, and supplying submergent and emergent vegetation for wetland restoration, environmental, and land reclamation concerns.

Kester's Wild Game Food Nurseries
PO Box 516
Omro, WI 54963
414-685-2929

Excellent source of seed, rootstock, and plants. Its catalog is packed with information and makes a good reference for wildlife attractants.

Lilypons Water Gardens
PO Box 10
Buckeystown, MD 21717
1-800-999-5459

Good selection of aquatics for natural ponds. The color photos are excellent.

Prairie Ridge Nursery
9738 Overland Road
Mount Horeb, WI 53572-2832
608-437-5245

Propagated native plants and seeds for prairies, woodlands, and wetlands. Offers a wide variety of grasses and sedges for upland cover, as well as aquatics.

William Tricker, Inc.
7125 Tanglewood Drive
Independence, OH 44131
1-800-524-3492

Shallow-water and bog plants with color photos. Also, a large selection of plants for water gardens.

Wildlife Nurseries, Inc.
PO Box 2794
Oshkosh, WI 54903-2724
414-231-3780

Wetland seeds and plants to attract wildlife, as well as mallard nesting cylinders and wood-duck boxes. Exceptionally informative catalog with planting techniques and suggestions. Seeds and plant stocks to attract waterfowl and other wildlife. A good source of plants for landscape architects and water gardeners, too. Nice selection of seeds, roots, and tubers for wetland improvement.

Fiberglass Nesting Baskets for Waterfowl

Hanson Manufacturing Inc.
PO Box 536
Turtle Lake, ND 58575
701-448-2593

Kenco Plastics
PO Box 39
Necedah, WI 54646
608-565-2203

Raven Industries
PO Box 1007
Sioux Falls, SD 57101
605-336-2750

Mallard Cylinder Nests

Cattail Products, Ltd.
PO Box 309
Fulton, IL 61252
815-589-4230

BOOKS AND OTHER PUBLICATIONS

Getting Food from Water
Gene Logsdon
Rodale Press
33 East Main Street
Emmaus, PA

Excellent all-round treatment of aquatic management, including ponds for wildlife. Out of print; check your library.

Land and Water Magazine
PO Box 1197
Fort Dodge, IA 50501-9925
515-576-3191

Solid information on the latest techniques in water management and aquatic landscaping, including occasional articles on wetland construction and management. Good source of industry professionals.

Landscaping for Wildlife
Carrol L. Henderson
Minnesota Department of Natural Resources
500 Lafayette Road, Box 7
St. Paul, MN 55155-4007

A thorough, beautifully illustrated guide to creating habitat for all sorts of wildlife, including waterfowl. While the focus is on animals and plants native to the northern Midwest, the principles apply around the country. Order this book from Minnesota's Bookstore: 1-800-657-3757

Management of Wood Ducks on Private Lands and Waters
Publication 420-802
Virginia Cooperative Extension Service
Extension Distribution Center
112 Landsdown Street
Blacksburg, VA 24061-0512
540-231-6192

Native Vegetation for Lakeshores, Streamsides, and Wetland Buffers
Vermont Agency of Natural Resources
103 South Main Street
Waterbury, VT 05671-0408
802-241-3770

How to establish shoreline trees and shrubs and plants to provide cover and food for wildlife. Planting techniques and species suggestions. A good illustrated guidebook designed for Vermont, but of value throughout much of the Northeast.

Nest Structures for Ducks and Geese
Iowa Department of Natural Resources
Wallace State Office Building
Des Moines, IA 50319-0034
515-281-5918

Waterfowl Habitat Management Handbook for the Lower Mississippi River Valley
Ducks Unlimited, Mississippi Cooperative Extension Service, National Fish and Wildlife Foundation
Available from Ducks Unlimited
One Waterfowl Way
Memphis, TN 38120
901-758-3825

Waterscaping
by Judy Glattstein
Storey Communications
Schoolhouse Road
Pownal, VT 05261
1-800-441-5700

A superior all-around guide to water gardening, with plenty of information on plants for natural ponds, including historical background and design schemes.

Wetlands: A National Audubon Society Guide
by William A. Niering
Alfred A. Knopf
201 East 50th Street
New York, NY 10022
1-800-733-3000

Terrific reference book with lots of entries for plants attractive to waterfowl and other water-loving critters. One of the bibles of the environmental movement.

EARTH PONDS VIDEO

Wildlife Harvest Magazine
PO Box 96
Goose Lake, IA 52750
319-242-3046

Magazine for game bird production and hunting. Good digest of current activities and source of information for pond owners who want to stock or to attract waterfowl or to create a wetland hunting habitat. Interesting ads and reprints. Editor John Mullin reminded me that people who raise hunting dogs like to have ponds for them to train in, and cool off.

Woodworking for Wildlife
by Carrol L. Henderson
Minnesota Department of Natural Resources
500 Lafayette Road, Box 7
St. Paul, MN 55155-4007
Order from Minnesota's Bookstore
1-800-652-9747

A top-notch guide to building nesting boxes and platforms for many kinds of birds, including ducks, geese, and even loons. Glossy four-color photos of the birds, easy-to-follow construction plans, and well-informed profiles of each bird make this one of my favorite how-to books. The spiral binding makes it convenient to read and use the building plans. Highly recommended.

ORGANIZATIONS

Ducks Unlimited
One Waterfowl Way
Memphis, TN 38120
901-758-3825

If you're serious about attracting waterfowl, you'll probably want to join Ducks Unlimited, if not for its emphasis on hunting techniques, then for its information about habitat improvement. In addition to publishing a bimonthly magazine, Ducks Unlimited runs a waterfowl conservation research program. A good outfit to get acquainted with.

North American Loon Fund
6 Lily Pond Road
Gilford, NH 03246
603-528-4711

Offers information and products related to loon preservation, including loon nesting platform plans. Membership newsletter.

Beaver management

Beaver Traps, Control Structures, and Repellents

Agri Drain Corporation
PO Box 458
1491 340th Street
Adair, IA 50002
1-800-232-4742

Supplies, plastic intakes, Control Structures™, and bar guards to protect pipe inlets. A comprehensive catalog of piping equipment and accessories of interest to pond owners and contractors.

C.E. Shepherd Co., Inc.
PO Box 9445
Houston, TX 77261-9445
1-800-324-6733

Corrosion-resistant steel wire mesh for protection against predators.

Forestry Suppliers, Inc.
PO Box 8397
Jackson, MS 39284-8397
1-800-647-5368

Tomahawk live traps and Conibear lethal traps.

The Hancock Live Trap
Box 268
Custer, SD 57730
605-673-4128

Recommended by beaver rights advocates as the best live beaver trap on the market. Otter model also available.

Plow and Hearth
PO Box 5000
Madison, VA 22727
1-800-627-1712

Sells Ropel, a nonlethal chemical beaver repellent recommended for use on vulnerable trees. It may be effective when used on beaver scent mounds to confuse the animal's territorial marking.

BOOKS & OTHER PUBLICATIONS

The American Beaver
by Lewis H. Morgan
Dover Publications, Inc.
31 East Second Street
Mineola, NY 11501
1-800-223-3130

Originally published in 1868, Morgan's The American Beaver *became a classic nature study, and continues in print today. Combining beaver lore and direct observation, the author portrays a world of wetlands and stream ecosystems, trappers and Native Americans, with the beaver at the center. Why are humans so fascinated by beavers? As Morgan puts it: "The results of the persevering labors of the beaver were suggestive of human industry." An in-depth look at beaver anatomy, dams, ledges, burrows, canals, meadows, trails, subsistence, and trapping. Fascinating history and an appealing prose style make this a compelling book for beaverphiles and pond owners alike.*

Baffling Beavers: Solutions to Beaver Flooding Problems
compiled by Phyllis A. Bellmore
PO Box 40
Plainfield, NH 03781

Plans, materials, and costs for a variety of beaver-foiling devices are laid out in this short manual. Bellmore is a beaver rights champion, and she has collected plans for solving problems in culverts and ponds, both man-made and beaver-made. She cites the success of the Canadian government in designing Beaver Stops for its provincial parks, although no address is given for ordering materials.

Beaver: Water Resources and Riparian Habitat Manager
by Olsen and Hubert
University of Wyoming
Publications Department
Laramie, WY 82071
307-766-1121

Excellent beaver management pamphlet accenting western problems and solutions.

Beaver Men
by Mari Sandoz
University of Nebraska Press
Lincoln, NE 68588
401-472-7211

Essential reading for anyone interested in the history of beavers in North America, especially the beaver trade and how it "fired the appetite for empire in the great courts of Europe and dictated foreign policy over much of America and Europe, so long as the beaver lasted." Full of lore and history; a classic originally published in 1964.

Beavers
by James E. Miller and Greg K. Yarrow
USDA, APHIS, ADC
Natural Resources and Rural Development Unit
Washington, DC 20250
301-734-8281

Damage prevention and control, including a detailed section on trapping.

ORGANIZATIONS

Beavers, Wetlands & Wildlife
Box 591
Little Falls, NY 13365
518-568-2077
Publishes educational materials and the Beaverspite Newsletter. *A membership-subscription is $15 and up.*

Unexpected Wildlife Refuge, Inc.
PO Box 765
Newfield, NJ 08344
609-697-3541
Publishes educational materials and The Beaver Defenders Newsletter. *A membership-subscription is $10 per year.*

US Department of Agriculture, Animal and Plant Health Inspection Service, Animal Damage Control

Every state has a USDA/APHIS office, which is a good source of information about animal damage control, beavers included. However, APHIS has no legal jurisdiction; for that, you'll have to check your state Fish and Wildlife Department. Through these sources you may be able to track down people who supply beaver baffles, and perhaps trappers who can remove the beavers.

Wildlife 2000
PO Box 6428
Denver, CO 80206
303-935-4995

Wildlife conservation outfit specializing in live trapping and/or relocating beavers in Colorado. Publishes an informative newsletter for members.

Attracting amphibians

Zetts Fish Farm and Hatcheries
Drifting, PA 16834
814-345-5357

"Giant Jumbo" bullfrog tadpoles and mixed species of turtles available from this fish farm, founded in 1900.

BOOKS & OTHER PUBLICATIONS

The Frog Book
by Mary C. Dickerson
Dover Publications
31 East Second Street
Mineola, NY 11501
1-800-223-3130

This nature study classic will tell you more than you ever wanted to know about frogs and toads, and make you glad you learned. Check out the parallels between plant bud size and the peeper song cycle. If you've got a pond without frogs, it's not a pond.

Getting Food from Water
by Gene Logsdon
Rodale Press
33 East Main Street
Emmaus, PA

A good section on frog farming in an excellent book about all aspects of backyard aquaculture. Out of print, try your library.

Pond Life
by Barbara Taylor
DK Publishing, Inc.
1224 Heil Quaker Blvd.
La Vergne, TN 37086

Good reference geared toward children; excellent close-up photographs.

The Professional Turtle Harvest
by C. Check
The Real Outdoors Co.
10422 North Road
Tomahawk, WI 54487
715-453-4225

Turtle history, trapping, butchering, and marketing. Did you know that turtle soup was one of Campbell's originals?

Wetlands

BOOKS & OTHER PUBLICATIONS

Constructed Wetlands for Wastewater Treatment and Wildlife Habitat
Environmental Protection Agency
Superintendent of Documents
PO Box 371954
Pittsburgh, PA 15250-7954
202-512-1800

Seventeen case studies of wastewater-treatment wetlands, highlighting operational experience and research results. Written in language accessible to the general public, this guide contains one of the best explanations I've seen. Illustrated with charts and photographs, a primer for individuals and organizations considering the merits of these systems.

Creating Fresh Water Wetlands
by Donald Hammer
Lewis Publishers/CRC Press, Inc.
2000 Corporate Blvd., N.W.
Boca Raton, FL 33431
407-998-9114

Land and Water Magazine
PO Box 1197
Fort Dodge, IA 50501-9925
515-576-3191

Some of the best articles I've read about how constructed wetlands are designed and built, and how they perform. Stories by Corps of Engineers personnel as well as private and state engineers. Although the magazine is not exclusively devoted to wetland design, you'll find a lot on the subject.

Living on Flood Plains and Wetlands: A Homeowner's Handbook
by Maureen Gilmer
Taylor Publishing Company
1550 West Mockingbird Lane
Dallas, TX 75235
Available from The Terrene Institute (see below).

How to live in a wetland as well as create one, and information on all matters aquatic. Essential reading for wetland students.

Natural Systems for Waste Management and Treatment
by Reed, Crites, and Middlebrook
McGraw Hill
1221 Avenue of the Americas
New York, NY 10020
212-512-2000

The New Field Book of Freshwater Life
by Elsie B. Klots
G.P. Putnam & Sons
111835 Olympic Boulevard
East Tower, Suite 500
Los Angeles, CA 90064
310-477-6100

Good field guide to pond life, from algae to alligators.

EARTH PONDS VIDEO

Pond and Brook: A Guide to Nature in Freshwater Environments
by Michael J. Caduto
University Press of New England
Hanover, NH 03755

Excellent introduction to freshwater environments, from wetlands and deep lakes to streams and vernal pools. Designed for the amateur naturalist.

Pond Life
by George K. Reid
Golden Books Publishing Co., Inc.
850 Third Avenue
New York, NY 10022
1-800-558-5972

Classic, pocket-sized, full-color guide to pond critters and plants. A must for any pond owner who wants a quick and easy identification book. Especially good for kids.

Pondwatchers Guide to Ponds and Vernal Pools of Eastern North America
Massachusetts Audubon Society
208 South Great Road
Lincoln, MA 01773
617-259-9506

Vivid full-color, laminated, fold-out eight-sided guide to pond life. More than 60 species of amphibians, reptiles, invertebrates, and plants found in permanent and temporary ponds. Good weather-resistant companion for a field trip; excellent for kids and students.

Wetland Planting Guide for the Northeastern United States
by Gwendolyn A. Thunhorst
Environmental Concern, Inc.
210 West Chew Avenue
St. Michaels, MD 21663
410-745-9620

Comprehensive guide to plants for wetland creation, restoration, and enhancement. Includes details on wildlife benefits, planting suggestions, and drawings. Excellent.

ORGANIZATIONS

EAP Industries, Inc.
Environmental Services Division
100 Blockdale Street, Watercrest Plaza
Sheswick, PA 15024
412-274-0700

Provides wetland design services.

International Wetlands for the Americas
PO Box 1770
Mahomet, MA 02345
508-224-6524

Wetland advocacy organization.

Michigan Wildlife Habitat Foundation
6380 Drumheller Road
P.O. Box 393
Bath, MI 48808
517-641-7677

Focuses on wildlife habitat for Michigan landowners, but publishes a newsletter of interest to all wetland stewards. $25 membership.

Ocean Arks International
233 Hatchville Road
East Falmouth, MA 02536
508-563-2792

Designs treatment systems based on natural wetland processes.

The Terrene Institute
4 Herbert Street
Alexandria, VA 22305
703-548-5473

Environmental education is its forté, and besides Lake Smarts *(reviewed on page 57) the institute publishes and distributes books, fact sheets, and posters relating to wetlands.*

US Fish and Wildlife Service
Refuges and Wildlife
4401 North Fairfax Drive
Arlington, VA 22203
703-358-2161

The US Fish and Wildlife Service sponsors a program called Partners for Wildlife, which offers the resources and knowledge of wetland specialists to interested landowners and also sponsors that North American waterfowl management plan.

Wetland Training Institute
PO Box 31
Greenwood, NM 88039
877-792-6482

Wetlands International
7 Hinton Avenue
Ottawa, Ontario K1Y 4P1
Canada
613-722-2090

Environmental Protection Agency

Wetlands hotline 1-800-832-7828

Region I: CT, MA, ME, NH RI, VT
Wetlands Protection Section (WWP-1900)
US EPA—Region I
John F. Kennedy Federal Building
Boston, MA 02203-1911
617-565-4421; fax: 617-565-4940

Region II: NJ, NY, PR, VI
Wetlands Protection Section (2WM-MWP)
US EPA—Region II
26 Federal Plaza, Room 837
New York, NY 10278
212-264-5170; fax: 212-264-4690

Region III: DE, MD, PA, VA, WV
Wetlands Protection Section (3ES42)
US EPA—Region III
841 Chestnut Street
Philadelphia, PA 19107
215-597-9301; fax: 215-597-1850

Region IV: AL, FL, GA, KY, MS, NC, SC, TN
Wetlands Regulatory Section
US EPA—Region IV
345 Courtland Street N.E.
Atlanta, GA 30365
404-347-4015; fax: 404-347-3269

Region V: IL, IN, MI, MN, OH, WI
Wetlands and Watersheds Section (WQW-16J)
US EPA—Region V
77 West Jackson Boulevard
Chicago, IL 60604
312-886-0243; fax: 312-886-7804

Region VI: AR, LA, NM, OK, TX
Wetlands Protection Section (6E-FT)
US EPA—Region VI
1445 Ross Avenue, Suite 900
Dallas, TX 75202
214-655-2263; fax: 214-655-7446

Region VII: IA, KS, MO, NE
Wetlands Protection Section (ENRV)
US EPA—Region VII
726 Minnesota Avenue
Kansas City, KS 66101
913-551-7573; fax: 913-551-7863

Region VIII; CO, MT, ND, SD, UT, WY
Wetlands Protection Section
(8WM-WQ)
US EPA—Region VIII
999 18th Street, 500 Denver Place
Denver, CO 80202-2405
303-293-1570; fax: 303-391-6957

Region IX: AZ, CA, HI, NV, Pacific Islands
Wetlands and Coastal Planning Section
(W-7-4)
US EPA—Region IX
75 Hawthorne Street
San Francisco, CA 94105
415-744-1971; fax: 415-744-1078

Region X: AK, ID, OR, WA
Wetlands Section (WD-128)
US EPA—Region X
1200 Sixth Avenue
Seattle, WA 98101
206-553-1412; fax: 206-553-1775

US Army Corps of Engineers Division Offices—Regulatory Program

US Army Corps of Engineers
Lower Mississippi Valley Division
(CELMV-CO-R)
PO Box 80
Vicksburg, MS 39180-0080
601-634-5818

US Army Corps of Engineers
Missouri River Division
(CEMRD-CO-R)
PO Box 103, Downtown Station
Omaha, NE 68101-0103
402-221-7290

US Army Corps of Engineers
New England Division
(CENED-OD-P)
424 Trapelo Road
Waltham, MA 02254-9149
617-647-8057

US Army Corps of Engineers
North Atlantic Division
(CENAD-CO-OP)
90 Church Street
New York, NY 10007-9998
212-264-7535

US Army Corps of Engineers
North Central Division
(CENCD-CO-MO)
536 South Clark Street
Chicago, IL 60605-1592
312-353-6379

US Army Corps of Engineers
North Pacific Division
(CENPD-CO-R)
PO Box 2870
Portland, OR 97208-2870
503-326-3780

US Army Corps of Engineers
Ohio River Division
(CEORD-CO-OR)
PO Box 1159
Cincinnati, OH 45201-1159
513-684-3972

US Army Corps of Engineers
Pacific Ocean Division
(CEPOD-CO-O)
Building 230
Fort Shafter, HI 96858-5440
808-438-9258

US Army Corps of Engineers
South Atlantic Division
(CESAD-CO-R)
Room 313
77 Forsythe Street SW
Atlanta, GA 30335-6801
404-331-2778

US Army Corps of Engineers
South Pacific Division
(CESPD-CO-O)
630 Sansome Street, Room 1216
San Francisco, CA 94111-2206
415-705-1443

US Army Corps of Engineers
Southwestern Division
(CESWD-CO-R)
1114 Commerce Street
Dallas, TX 75242-0216
214-767-2432

United States Fish and Wildlife Service

The following regional offices may be able to offer information regarding wetland construction.

Headquarters
US Fish and Wildlife Service
Department of the Interior
1849 C Street, NW
Washington, DC 20240

Region 1: CA, HI, ID, NV, OR, WA
US Fish and Wildlife Service
Eastside Federal Complex
911 NE 11th Avenue
Portland, OR 97232-4181
503-231-6118

Region 2: AZ, NM, OK, TX
US Fish and Wildlife Service
500 Gold Avenue, SW
Albuquerque, NM 87103
505-766-2321

Region 3: IL, IN, IA, MI, MN, MO, OH, WI
US Fish and Wildlife Service
Whipple Federal Building
Fort Snelling, MN 55111-4056
612-725-3563

Region 4: AL, AR, FL, GA, KY, LA, MS, NC, SC, TN
US Fish and Wildlife Service
1875 Century Boulevard, #410
Atlanta, GA 30345-3301
404-679-4000

Region 5: CT, DE, MA, MD, ME, NH, NJ, NY, PA, RI, VT, VA, WV
US Fish and Wildlife Service
300 Westgate Center Drive
Hadley, MA 01035-9589
413-253-8200

Region 6: KS, MO, NE, ND, SD, UT, WY
US Fish and Wildlife Service
134 Union Boulevard
Lakewood, CO 80228
303-236-7920

Region 7: Alaska
US Fish and Wildlife Service
1011 East Tudor Road
Anchorage, AK 99503
907-786-3542

5. GARDEN PONDS

In my line of work, it's not unusual to run into people with lots of ambition but not much water. Instead of wasting money on a pond that won't fill up, I used to suggest they consider a swimming pool. Now I propose building a garden pond. It's less expensive than a swimming pool, and offers many of the rewards of a full-sized pond: wildlife attraction, landscape improvement, and a place to raise fish and aquatic plants. Not a bad trade-off, considering that you can do it all yourself, from excavation to installation.

In fact, garden pond construction is booming, spurred by an ever-increasing appetite for household improvement projects, new construction materials, and a proliferation of water garden suppliers offering a large variety of water lilies and other aquatic plants. Although this may seem like a new trend in landscaping, it's actually an old tradition revisited. The ancient Romans built fountains and stair-step pools to refresh their sun-baked cities, and in medieval Japan sophisticated water gardens were designed and built to reflect spiritual beliefs. The Victorian English built palatial, glass-covered goldfish ponds.

Not long ago the phrase *garden pond* conjured up visions of a concrete square of water isolated within a formal outdoor setting. Think of Versailles. That all began to change with the popularity of West Coast–influenced landscaping, with its looser, natural look. And then about a decade ago, new materials—lightweight, preformed fiberglass pools and flexible plastic liners—made it possible to put a small pool just about anywhere.

Before you start digging, though, consider your objectives. A simple reflecting pool without fish or plants requires the least amount of planning. Adding fish or plants means giving more thought to materials, siting, and maintenance. And depending on your climate, you may have to design safeguards for overheating in summer or freezing in winter. It may be necessary to provide shade or supplemental water to keep temperatures down in hot weather; water circulators can also help. In winter, you may have to move plants to a lower level in the pool to prevent freezing, or remove them altogether. In extremely cold climates you may wish to drain and cover the pond to prevent icing damage. Be sure to check zoning laws regarding safety standards, such as fencing and warning signs.

COURTESY OF LILYPONS WATER GARDENS

Siting

Choosing the location is the most important step in pond construction. Most people prefer a place close to the house, where it can be seen, but a secluded pond can offer a tranquil retreat. If you have young children or pets, consider how they fit in the equation. Nobody wants kids getting hurt or dogs trampling on the $40 lotuses. Fencing may be necessary.

If you plan to grow aquatic plants, sunlight is important. Lilies like about six hours of sun daily. However, too much heat can be lethal to fish, so you may want to provide shade from the afternoon sun. Avoid sites too close to trees, which can litter the pond with leaves and cause damage to the liner with their roots. Windy sites should be avoided to prevent damage to aquatic plants.

A level, well-drained site is essential. If a slope has to be leveled off for the pond, be sure that terrain alteration won't collect rainfall or funnel runoff into the pond. Ditches, berms, terraces, and drainage tiles will deflect runoff from entering the pond. Most garden ponds are filled with household water, which is kept healthy by oxygenating plants and/or a circulation and filtration system, and scavengers such as snails, frogs, and fish. Except for small amounts added to make up for evaporation, they do not require an exchange of fresh water. However, an outlet channel for overflow may be necessary to take care of rainfall. Avoid soggy locations with a high water table, where groundwater can get under pond liners and lift them up. When in doubt, dig a test pit to be sure your water table won't threaten the liner.

The site should be free of any underground electric or utility lines. Probe the site with an auger or pry bar to determine if you'll have problems with rocks or ledge. And make plans for the excavated soil, distributing it where it won't wash back into the pond.

Pond size will depend on the size of your yard and your ambitions. A balanced living environment for plants and fish requires a larger pond, roughly 40 square feet of surface area or more. For each square foot of surface, you should aim for 10 gallons of water. A cubic foot of water contains only 7.5 gallons, so depths closer to 2 feet are recommended. If you plan to grow bog plants, include a shallow shelf around the edge of the pond, which can also serve as a safety measure for children.

Material

Next, you'll want to choose the pond material. Today most ponds are made with either rigid, preformed fiberglass or plastic, or a flexible liner. Preformed ponds are available in a variety of shapes and sizes, although I've heard some complaints that they tend to be too shallow to sustain stable temperatures. Preformed pools range in depth from less than a foot to 2 feet, depending upon overall size. The shallowest pools may be unsatisfactory. Eighteen inches is a safe minimum. Flexible liners are constructed of ultraviolet-resistant PVC plastic or butyl rubber, and can be worked into whatever shape required. Water-garden suppliers offer liners of varying thicknesses, from 20 millimeters up to as much as 60. The thicker the liner, the more durable, and some of the better materials come with a lifetime guarantee against leakage. Manufacturers offer formulas for calculating liner size to match the excavation. Professionals appear to favor flexible liners because of their versatility.

Whatever material you choose, be sure to outline the perimeter of your imaginary pond to see how it fits the site. A length of garden hose makes a good visualization tool.

Installation

Once you've decided on materials and shape, outline the perimeter and dig in. Try to dig when the soil is easiest to work, neither heavy with rain nor so dry that it won't hold an edge. Whether you use a pick and shovel or a backhoe, one tool is a must: a reliable level. You may have to mount the level on a 2-by-4 to span the excavation. If you don't keep the edges level, you'll wind up with excess liner on the high side showing over the waterline. The level will also enable you to establish a uniform pool depth, by measuring down at various points.

Whether you're using a preformed pool or flexible membrane, remove all sharp rocks to prevent puncture. For a flexible liner, dig the hole at about a 75-degree angle to prevent slumping. The sidewall angle is determined by the quality of soil. The sandier the soil, the more likely it is to slump; thus, the angle must be flatter. In extremely sandy soil you may have to reinforce the walls with concrete blocks; in that case you can have 90-degree side walls. Most liner manufacturers recommend using a layer of sand and/or underlayment beneath the material to protect the material from puncture. An inch or two of sand, old carpet, geotextile, or even cardboard or newspaper makes a good buffer. In the case of a squared-off excavation reinforced with concrete blocks, rigid Styrofoam insulation over the concrete offers protection.

Creating a Garden Pool

1.

Outline the pool perimeter with a rope or garden hose. (For a rectangle or square, use strings, stakes, and a carpenter's square.) Dig just inside the perimeter, leaving room for edging material. A wheelbarrow or truck is helpful for moving soil. Be sure not to pile excavated earth near the pool edge.

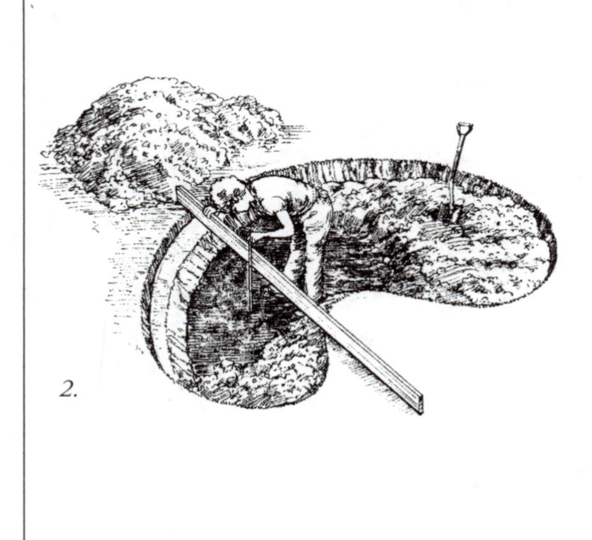

2.

As you dig, include shelves if desired. Shelves should be about 9 inches wide and 9 to 12 inches below the top edge. Use a straight board and level to make sure the edges are level and the bottom depth is uniform.

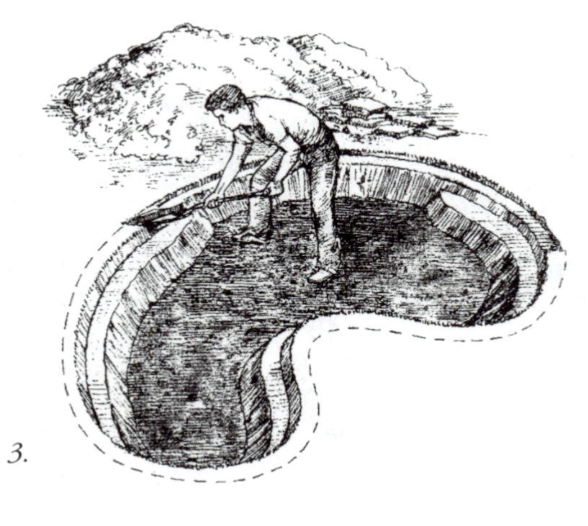

3.

A shallow 12- to 15-inch wide ledge should be cut back from the edge for any intended coping, or edging, material. The bottom should be gradually sloped to one end to facilitate cleaning. Make sure no rocks or sharp objects remain. Sand and/or polyethylene plastic sheeting can be used to further cushion the liner.

4.

Drape the liner over the excavation (it will be more pliable if allowed to warm up in the sun briefly), and anchor with stones or bricks. As you introduce water, the weights can be removed as the liner drops into place.

5.

After filling, trim the overlapping edge to 1 foot, fold up an inch or so to catch overflow, and anchor with large galvanized nails.

6.

Secure the edge with stone, brick, or other coping material. The coping material should overlap the liner an inch or two to protect against ultraviolet deterioration.

DRAWINGS BY ELAYNE SEARS, COURTESY OF LILYPONS WATER GARDENS

Install a flexible liner on a warm sunny day, so that the liner can heat up in the sun long enough to become pliable (but not so long that it burns your lawn grass underneath). The liner should be laid so that it overlaps the hole, with stones anchoring the edges. Then slowly introduce the water. As the pond fills, it's important to work the material to ease out folds and wrinkles. After filling, trim the overlapping edge to 1 foot, fold up an inch or so to catch overflow, and anchor with large nails. Stones, bricks, or other coping material is then used over the edge.

Preformed ponds don't require the same degree of custom fitting, although you may have to touch up the excavation to make sure the structure rests uniformly on the ground. To prevent damage to the pool, the hole should be backfilled periodically as the water rises. Most garden ponds do not include a drain, and draining for cleaning, repairs, or overwintering is usually accomplished with either a siphon hose or a pump.

Planting

Once the garden pond is filled, let the water stand for a couple of days to dissipate chemicals, especially if the water is treated with chlorine. Check that the pH is between 6.5 and 7.5. Garden supply outfits as well as water gardening and aquacultural suppliers sell test kits for determining pH. Higher readings forecast an alga problem, which can be averted by the addition of vinegar. With a concrete pool, you'll want to fill and drain the structure several times over a period of two weeks to flush out potentially toxic chemicals.

If you're growing plants exclusively, aim for a balanced community of floating, submerged, and bog plants. Lilies and lotuses, with their large floating leaves, provide the shade necessary to moderate temperatures and discourage algae. Two-thirds of the surface area in such shade is the standard recommendation. Submerged plants such as elodea and eelgrass add necessary oxygen. Bog plants—arrowhead and pitcher plants, for example—help take up potentially damaging nutrients. In fact, during the first few weeks after stocking your pond with plants, you may notice a burst of alga growth. Water-gardening experts unanimously advise against treating the water with chemicals or draining the pond to clean up. This sudden growth of algae is a natural occurrence before the plants begin to coexist, and should soon subside.

Ornamentals

Nothing symbolizes the beauty of a water garden better than a fragrant water lily in full bloom. Water lilies and their kindred lotuses have charmed people for centuries, dating back to the ancient Chinese and Japanese, who envisioned their ponds as earthly counterparts to paradise. Later, Greek legends tell of the Lotophagi, lotus-eaters whose diet enabled them to transcend worldly worries. Today, glossy color catalogs from water-garden nurseries have a similar effect, arriving in winter to help people forget the cold and indulge in daydreams of pools resplendent with purple and mauve.

Hardy perennial water lilies offer a wide spectrum of

trouble-free plants. Most hardy water lilies can overwinter in 24 inches of water, as long as the tubers don't freeze. In severe climates, root the plants in containers and take them indoors for the winter. To encourage maximum flowering, it's important not to overcrowd them. About a third of the water surface should be free of plant leaves. Water lilies like still water and sun; the more sun, the more flowers. They also like monthly infusions of fertilizer during flowering. Many water-garden suppliers sell fertilizer tablets, which are inserted into the soil in the plant container. The amount of fertilizer depends on the plant species and the amount of soil in the container. For plants in earth-bottomed ponds, estimate the size of the soil block around the plant roots to determine how much fertilizer you'll need.

Planting in spring or early summer is usually done in containers supported just a few inches below the water surface, where the water is warmest. After the plants have established themselves, they can be set at the bottom, where they can also overwinter.

Tropical water lilies are most often grown as annuals. They offer more profuse blooms and stronger fragrances, and some varieties bloom at night. Lotuses develop leaves and flowers that stand above the water. These perennials take longer to become established; some require a year or two before they'll bloom.

To create a balanced environment in a garden pond, it's important to include submerged plants like elodea and free-floating plants like water hyacinth, water lettuce, duckweed, and water aloe.

Where space is a problem, it's possible to create a mini-pond in a container of some sort. Polyethylene tubs are available from most water-garden suppliers; half whiskey barrels, claw-foot bathtubs, hot tubs, and decorative ceramics also will do. Many of the plants discussed can be used on a smaller scale. Starting out with a container is also a good way to give the garden pond concept a low-budget tryout. (See Planting for Wildlife, page 115–20, for more suggestions about landscaping around ponds.)

Fish Ponds

Fish are a traditional part of the garden pond population, although they may present some difficulties. Popular varieties such as goldfish and koi may feed on expensive plants as they grow larger, and the food it takes to keep them alive often becomes waste matter that nourishes algae, especially if the fish are overfed. You may need mechanical filters to keep the water clean. In cold climates fish may have to be taken in during the winter; they can also make a tasty meal for predatory birds and animals. Fish do have the advantage of keeping down the mosquito population, however, and they're pretty to look at.

Backyard fish ponds can be built with earth, wood, flexible rubber or plastic liners, poured-on preformed concrete that has been waterproofed, preformed fiberglass rolls, and miscellaneous containers like ceramic pots, crocks, old bathtubs, beer kegs, plastic tubs, and 55-gallon steel drums. Aboveground pools and translucent solar storage tubes are also used to raise warm-water fish for the table. If you are using earth, either it has to be clay rich to hold water, or you will have to use a soil sealer to keep the pool or pond from leaking. Wood in the form of half-barrels or crates can be waterproofed if necessary with paint or a plastic sealer. Choose the material that fits your site, your budget, and the kind of fish you want to raise.

Currently, decorative-pond makers appear to favor two materials. The first, a flexible liner, is usually PVC or synthetic rubber. A black liner is better than either the translucent or the blue, because of its natural look. The other preferred material is a preformed fiberglass pool. They come in many shapes and sizes, and since they are formed in one piece, there is little chance of leakage.

Both liners and preformed fiberglass pools have a life span of 20 years or more. A 4-foot by 6-foot by 15-inch-deep preformed fiberglass pool costs about $350; a PVC liner for a similar-sized pool will run about $100. After the pool is excavated and the liner or pool installed, a shorebelt should be added to the rim. This can be sod, topsoil, rocks, flagstone, paving squares, or wood decking. Once the pool is filled, it may require flushing and refilling to decontaminate the liner, depending on the material. Finally, after fish are stocked, the pool keeper must maintain an environment that supports the fish. This usually means stocking plants to absorb carbon dioxide and add oxygen, supplying scavengers such as snails and frogs to help clean up detritus, and perhaps providing spawning mats where the fish can reproduce. Plants, scavengers, and spawning mats are available from water-garden suppliers.

Two members of the carp family, goldfish and koi, are the most popular ornamental fish stocked in garden ponds. Goldfish should be stocked at a rate of no more than 1 inch per 3 to 5 gallons of water; koi no more than ½ inch for the same amount. Although generally dependent on regular feedings—the highlight of the day for many fish fanciers—the fish are usually hardy enough to survive on submerged plants for a week or two. Fish should not be added to a new or newly filled pond until some vegetation has been introduced and established, which usually takes a couple of weeks. On the other hand, many experts recommend against mixing koi and valuable decorative plants, which they will eat. Koi as well as goldfish are also known for jumping out of fish ponds when stressed or during spawning. If this becomes a problem, the water level should be lowered 6 inches or so as a safeguard. It's also important to introduce fish to water with the same temperature they've been in. Float plastic bags containing new fish on the pond until the temperatures equalize, and then you can add the fish.

In my admittedly limited contact with water gardeners (I tend to hang out with people who like to dig big holes), I've noticed two kinds of pool people: the ones who are mad about plants, water lilies in particular, and the fish lovers. Helen Nash, one of the country's most prolific and respected water-gardening authors and founder of *Water Gardening* magazine, belongs to the former group. The Latin names for rare water lilies roll off her tongue, and she knows many of the venerable horticulturalists who hybridized them. I get the feeling that acquiring a rare water lily must be as thrilling as buying a Picasso, with the bonus that it's alive and provides its own perfume.

On the other hand, there are the fish lovers. I had a call from a woman in Pennsylvania not long ago, asking for advice about enlarging her pond so she could give her koi more space. I know enough about koi to appreciate their dazzling variety of colors and patterns, much like living fractals. In Japan, koi are venerated for their distinguished patterns and can be extremely valuable. I mentioned that it must be pleasant having a pool full of swimming jewels. Oh no, she replied, she saw her koi more like Hell's Angels. Their spectacular hues suggested gang colors, and they slunk around the pond like sullen Harley riders. She saw them as outlaws, and she loved it. They needed more room! At that moment I learned something about ponds—all ponds—that explains the special relationship people have with their backyard reservoirs. Ponds allow you to enlarge your dreams. It's that simple and that profound.

Resources

PRODUCTS & SUPPLIERS

The following companies sell plants, pond materials, instructive materials, and miscellaneous garden pond paraphernalia; many also sell fish.

AquaMats
Meridian Systems
4041 Powder Mill Road, Suite 710
Calverton, MD 20705
301-937-1270

Bio-habitat technology used to increase water clarity and improve fish and plant habitat.

Aquascape Designs, Inc.
1002 Carolina Drive
West Chicago, IL 60185
1-800-306-6227

Water-gardening catalog and services designed for professional landscape designers and pool installers. Prefers to deal wholesale.

Bee Fork Water Gardens
PO Box 440037
Brentwood, MO 63144-0437
314-962-1583

Gilberg Perennial Farms
2906 Ossington Road
Glencoe, MO 63038
314-458-2033

No mail order.

Laguna Koi Ponds
20452 Laguna Canyon Road
Laguna Beach, CA 92651
714-494-5107

Lilypons Water Gardens
PO Box 10
Buckeystown, MD 21717-0010
1-800-999-5459

Maryland Aquatic Nurseries, Inc.
3427 North Furnace Rroad
Jarrettsville, MD 20184
410-692-2837

Moorehaven Water Gardens
3006 York Road
Everett, WA 98204
206-743-6888

Paradise Water Gardens
14 May Street
Whitman, MA 02382
1-800-955-0161

Perry's Water Garden
191 Leatherman Gap Road
Franklin, NC 28734
1-800-LILY-PAD

Scherer & Sons
104 Waterside Road
Northport, NY 11768
516-261-7432

Slocum Water Gardens
1101 Cypress Gardens Boulevard
Winter Haven, FL 33884
941-293-7151

William Tricker, Inc.
7125 Tanglewood Drive
Independence, OH 44131
1-800-524-3492

Van Ness Water Gardens
2460 North Euclid Avenue
Upland, CA 91786
909-982-2425

Waterford Gardens
74 East Allendale Road
Saddle River, NJ 07458
201-327-0721

White Flower Farm
PO Box 50
Litchfield, CT 06759
1-800-503-9624

PONDS & POND SUPPLIES

Patio Garden Ponds
PO Box 890402
Oklahoma City, OK 73189-0402
405-634-POND

Tetra Pond
3001 Commerce Street
Blacksburg, VA 24060
1-800-526-0650

Liners and Soil Sealants

C.I.M Industries, Inc.
94 Grove Street
Peterborough, NH 03458
1-800-543-3458

Liquid urethane rubber liner, which can be poured, sprayed, or rolled. One version is UL rated for fish culture and potable water.

Hecht Rubber Corporation
6161 Phillips Highway
Jacksonville, FL 32216
904-731-3401

Reef Industries
PO Box 750245
Houston, TX 77275-0245
1-800-231-2417

Liners, any size.

Reimer Waterscapes
RR 3, Box 34
Tillsonburg, Ontario H4G 4H3
Canada
519-842-6049

Resource Conservation
Technology, Inc.
2633 North Calvert Street
Baltimore, MD 21218
410-366-1146

Liners, any size.

Garden Pond Fountains

Beckett Water Gardens
2521 Willowbrook Road
Dallas, TX 75220-4420
214-357-6421

Custom Fountains, Inc.
901 East Hanna Avenue
Mason, OH 45040
513-398-5141

Little Giant Pump Co.
PO Box 12010
Oklahoma City, OK 73157
405-947-2511

BOOKS & OTHER PUBLICATIONS

The Complete Pond Builder: Creating a Beautiful Water Garden
by Helen Nash
Sterling Publishing Co., Inc.
387 Park Avenue South
New York, NY 10016
1-800-367-9692

Creating Your Own Water Garden
by Charles B. Thomas
Storey Communications
Schoolhouse Road
Pownal, VT 05261
1-800-441-5700

Pamphlet.

Gardening with Water
by James Van Sweden
Random House
201 East 50th Street
New York, NY 10022
1-800-726-0600

Japanese Gardens
by Mitchell Bring and Josse Wayembergh
McGraw Hill Book Co.
1221 Avenue of the Americas
New York, NY 10020
212-512-2000

Pond and Garden
1670 South 800 East
Zionsville, IN 46077
317-769-3278

The Pond Doctor
by Helen Nash
Sterling Publishing Co., Inc.
387 Park Avenue South
New York, NY 10016
1-800-367-9692

Pondkeeper Magazine
100 Whitetail Court
Duncansville, PA 16635
814-695-4325

Stonescaping: A Guide to Using Stone in Your Garden
by Jan Kowalczewski Whitner
Storey Communications
Schoolhouse Road
Pownal, VT 05261
1-800-441-5700

Good book on stonework, including its use in and around garden ponds.

Water Features for Small Gardens
by Francesca Grenoak
Trafalgar Square Publishing
North Pomfret, VT 05053
802-457-1911

Water Gardening Magazine
12029 Wicker Ave.
Cedar Lake, IN 46303
1-800-308-6157

New magazine; excellent source of ideas and supplies.

Water Gardens: A Harrowsmith *Gardener's Guide*
edited by David Archibald and Mary Patton
distributed by Firefly Books
Box 1338
Ellicott Station
Buffalo, NY 14205
1-800-387-5085

Water Gardens for Plants and Fish
by Charles B. Thomas
T.F.H. Publications
Available from Lilypons Water Gardens (for address, see page 160)

Water Gardens: How to Design, Install, Plant, and Maintain a Home Water Garden
by Jacqueline Heriteau and Charles B. Thomas
Houghton-Mifflin Co.
222 Berkeley Street
Boston, MA 02116
1-800-225-3362

Water in the Garden
by James Allison
Little Brown & Company
1271 Avenue of the Americas
New York, NY 10020
1-800-343-9204

Waterscaping
by Judy Glattstein
Storey Communications
Schoolhouse Road
Pownal, VT 05261
1-800-441-5700

Waterside Planting
by Philip Swindells
Sterling Publishing Co., Inc.
387 Park Avenue South
New York, NY 10016
1-800-367-9692

Water Gardening: Water Lilies and Lotuses
by Penny D. Slocum and Peter Robinson
Timber Press
133 SW Second Avenue, Suite 450
Portland, OR 97204-3527
1-800-327-5680

Considered by many garden pond experts to the most complete book on water lilies and lotuses, written by two of the world's leading water-gardening experts. Covers water garden design, construction, maintenance, and plants. Illustrations and four-color photographs.

The Aquatic Bookshop
PO Box 2150
Shingle Springs, CA 95682-2150
916-622-7157

Mail-order bookstore specializing in garden ponds and aquaculture. Extensive book list available.

ORGANIZATIONS

The National Pond Society
286 Village Parkway
Marietta, GA 30067
1-800-742-4701

Sponsors tours, offers information, and publishes Pondscapes, *dedicated to garden ponds, 10 times annually.*

WATER GARDENS TO VISIT

Brooklyn Botanic Garden
1000 Washington Avenue
Brooklyn, NY 11225
718-622-4433

Chicago Botanic Garden
Lake Cook Road, PO Box 400
Glencoe, IL 60022
847-835-5440

Denver Botanic Gardens
909 York Street
Denver, CO 80206
303-331-4000

Garden in the Woods
180 Hemenway Road
Framingham, MA 01701
508-877-6574

New England's premier wildflower showcase features 45 acres of wildflowers, ferns, shrubs, and trees, a lily pond and bog. Many endangered species on display. Plants available. Courses offered include wetland species identification and restoration.

Huntington Botanical Gardens
1151 Oxford Road
San Marino, CA 91108
818-405-2141

Longwood Gardens
PO Box 50
Kennett Square, PA 19348
610-388-6741

Mercer Arboretum and Botanic Garden
22306 Aldine Westfield Road
Humble, TX 77338
713-947-0248

Montreal Botanical Gardens
4101 Sherbrooke Street East
Montreal, Quebec H1X 2B2
Canada
514-872-1400

Missouri Botanical Garden
4344 Shaw Boulevard
St. Louis, MO 63110
314-577-5100

New York Botanical Garden
200th Street and Southern Boulevard
Bronx, NY 10458-5126
718-817-8705

US National Arboretum
3501 New York Avenue, NE
Washington, DC 20002
202-245-2726

INDEX

The Earth Ponds Library

"Tim Matson is the guru of ponds." —*Albany Times-Union*

***Earth Ponds**: The Country Pond Maker's Guide to Building, Maintenance, and Restoration,* the top-selling companion book to *The Earth Ponds Sourcebook*, gives more detailed information on pond construction. It may be found in bookstores or ordered directly from the publisher by calling 1-800-245-4151.

Also available, the **Earth Ponds Video** gives detailed on-site examples of how ponds are designed, built, and used. Running time is 48 minutes. For more information or to order the video, contact Tim Matson, The Earth Ponds Company, 288 Miller Pond Road, Thetford Center, Vermont 05075, (802) 333-9019.

Also from The Countryman Press

Books for Country Living

Backyard Livestock
Backyard Sugarin'
The New Complete Guide to Beekeeping
Living with Herbs
Perennials for the Backyard Gardener
The New England Herb Gardener
Reading the Forested Landscape
Wilderness Ethics